Aztalan
Mysteries of an Ancient Indian Town

Aztalan

Mysteries of an Ancient Indian Town

Robert A. Birmingham
Lynne G. Goldstein

Wisconsin Historical Society Press

Published by the
Wisconsin Historical Society Press

www.wisconsinhistory.org

Photographs identified with PH, WHi, or WHS are from the Society's collections; address
inquiries about such photos to the Visual Materials Archivist at the above address.

Printed in the United States of America
Designed by Roberta H. Couillard

28 27 26 25 24   4 5

Library of Congress Cataloging-in-Publication Data
        Birmingham, Robert A.
                Aztalan : mysteries of an ancient indian town/by Robert A.
        Birmingham and Lynne Goldstein.
                p. cm.
Includes bibliographical references and index.
ISBN 0-87020-362-2 (pbk. : alk. paper)
        1. Mississippian culture—Wisconsin—Aztalan State Park. 2. Excavations (Archaeology)—
Wisconsin—Aztalan State Park. 3. Aztalan Mounds (Wis.) 4. Aztalan State Park (Wis.) I.
Goldstein, Lynne. II. Title.
E99.M6815.B48 2005
977.5'85–dc22
2005031952

The activity that is the subject of this book has been financed in part with Federal funds from
the National Park Service, U.S. Department of the Interior. However, the contents and opin-
ions do not necessarily reflect the views or policies of the Department of the Interior.

This program receives Federal financial assistance for identification and protection of historic
properties. Under Title VI of the Civil Rights Act of 1964, Section 504 of the Rehabilitation
Act of 1973, and the Age Discrimination Act of 1975, as amended, the U.S. Department of the
Interior prohibits discrimination on the basis of race, color, national origin, disability or age in its
federally assisted programs. If you believe you have been discriminated against in any program,
activity, or facility as described above, or if you desire further information, please write to: Office
of Equal Opportunity, National Park Service, 1849 C Street, N.W., Washington, D.C. 20240

Front cover: Painting by Rob Evans, used with permission of the Kenosha Public Museum.
Back cover: Photograph by Joel Heiman

∞ The paper used in this publication meets the minimum requirements of the American
National Standard for Information Sciences—Permanence of Paper for Printed Library
Materials, ANSI Z39.48-1992.

Contents

Acknowledgments

M any institutions and individuals contributed assistance and advice in preparation of this book. Alex Barker (Milwaukee Public Museum), Thomas Emerson (University of Illinois–Urbana-Champaign), Robert Boszhardt (Mississippi Valley Archaeology Center), and John D. Richards (University of Wisconsin–Milwaukee) reviewed drafts and provided helpful comments and corrections. Diane Holliday of Tucson, Arizona provided copyediting services. Also contributing various forms of assistance were the Wisconsin Department of Natural Resources and Aztalan State Park, Susan Otto and the Milwaukee Public Museum, the Lake Mills-Aztalan Historical Society, Cahokia Mounds Historic Site, the University of Wisconsin–Milwaukee, Michigan State University, The Smithsonian Institution, Etowah Mounds Historic Site, University of Arkansas, Joan E. Freeman (retired, Wisconsin Historical Society Museum), Steve Stiegerwald of Lake Mills, Tom Davies (Aztalan State Park), Donald Gaff (Michigan State University), Jon Carroll (Michigan State University), and Woody Wallace (Earth Information Technology). A portion of the work described and included here was conducted with the support of National Science Foundation Grant #BCS 0004394 (Goldstein). Finally, we would like to thank the staffs of the Wisconsin Historical Society archives, library, museum, the Office of the State Archaeologist, and the WHS Press for providing innumerable services and resources.

Introduction

Figure A. Aztalan

In 1836, settlers to western Michigan Territory, now Wisconsin, made a discovery that would confound scholars and the public over the next century. Along the Crawfish River, fifty miles west of the new village of Milwaukee, the newcomers stumbled upon the burned ruins of a massive fortification enclosing flat-topped earthen mounds. These mounds appeared to be smaller versions of fine stone structures found in Mexico and Central America. It was dubbed the "Citadel" because it reminded settlers of an old fortress.

The discovery of the site, widely reported in newspapers of the day, posed a great mystery. Who built this "fortress"? American Indians of the region, recently removed by treaties, made no such structures. They had lived in small, modest villages. Further, no history had been developed for North America and the indigenous people left no records that could account for such places in the Midwest. Archaeology could not address the questions posed by the site since it would not develop as a formal discipline in the United States until the early twentieth century.

For these and other reasons, the settlers were reluctant to believe that native North Americans built these walls and mounds. Instead, the similarity of the site to the better known Aztec ruins in Mexico led to the conclusion that the Aztecs were involved and the site must be that of Aztalan or Aztlán, the Aztec northern homeland. The name stuck to the site although today it speaks only of nineteenth-century attitudes and knowledge and says nothing about the inhabitants of this great town.

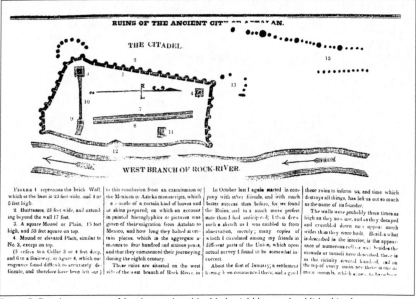

Figure B. First known map of Aztalan rendered by Nathaniel Hyer and published in the newspaper, *Milwaukee Advertiser* in 1837

As a result of archaeological work conducted throughout the twentieth century at Aztalan itself, archaeologists solved one mystery concerning the origin of the people who lived there. The large platform mounds and tens of thousands of artifacts found in the town link it to a remarkable civilization that archaeologists refer to as Mississippian. This civilization flourished between AD 1050 and the 1600s throughout the Mississippi River drainage, from Illinois to the Gulf Coast. The early capital of the Mississippian civilization was a large ceremonial, political, and urban center located near the Mississippi River in what is today, East St. Louis, in southern Illinois. In AD 1100, this exceptionally well-organized metropolis, complete with monumental architecture, supported a population variously estimated at 10,000–15,000 people. Archaeologists named this Indian city, Cahokia, after a later tribe that lived in the area. The actual name of the city is lost forever, but surely it once was known far and wide and perhaps even feared and revered.

Just prior to AD 1100, a group of Mississippians from Cahokia, or some other place in Cahokia's social sphere, migrated north to the Crawfish River in southern Wisconsin. Here they lived together with non-Mississippian groups, presumably friends, relatives, and allies. Together, these people lived at Aztalan for perhaps a century and a half. By AD 1250, the people had abandoned the town, foretelling the demise and eventual abandonment of Cahokia itself. By AD 1400, the Mississippian lifeway mysteriously disappeared from the Midwestern landscape, and the focus of the Mississippian civilization shifted to the southeastern United States.

The Mississippian newcomers reshaped the land along the Crawfish River into a characteristically well-organized Mississippian community. Huge timber and clay walls, supported by bastions or watchtowers, enclosed and subdivided the twenty-one acre town. Within the town, the people constructed three large earthen platform mounds and built important public buildings on top of each mound. All three building types could be found in later Mississippian communities in the southeastern United States. One platform mound at the northwest corner within the walled town supported a mortuary building or mausoleum where some members of the community were laid to rest. Another mound, located in the northeastern part of the town, appears to have been a public temple and council house, where a sacred fire was kept burning. On a high elevation at the southwest corner of the site, the Mississippians built the largest mound, upon which they erected a wooden pole structure that enclosed sacred space or probably the house of the chief along with the ruling family. In between the two large western mounds and the public residential district on the east, there was a large, level, and enclosed plaza where many of the social and ritual activities took place. At the north end of the plaza, the Mississippians maintained a special underground food storage area, probably for large public feasts and rituals.

An estimated 300–500 people lived at Aztalan at AD 1100. Pottery styles found throughout the town indicate that at least two different groups of people lived here: the Mississippians, perhaps from Cahokia itself, and many people referred to by archaeologists as Late Woodland, who inhabited southern Wisconsin and the Upper Midwest at this time.

The Mississippians and the people of Aztalan were principally corn farmers. Indeed, Aztalan can be called the first farming town in Wisconsin, a state that still defines its identity in terms of agriculture. An early settler's map indicates that at least some of the cornfields were on a level area just north

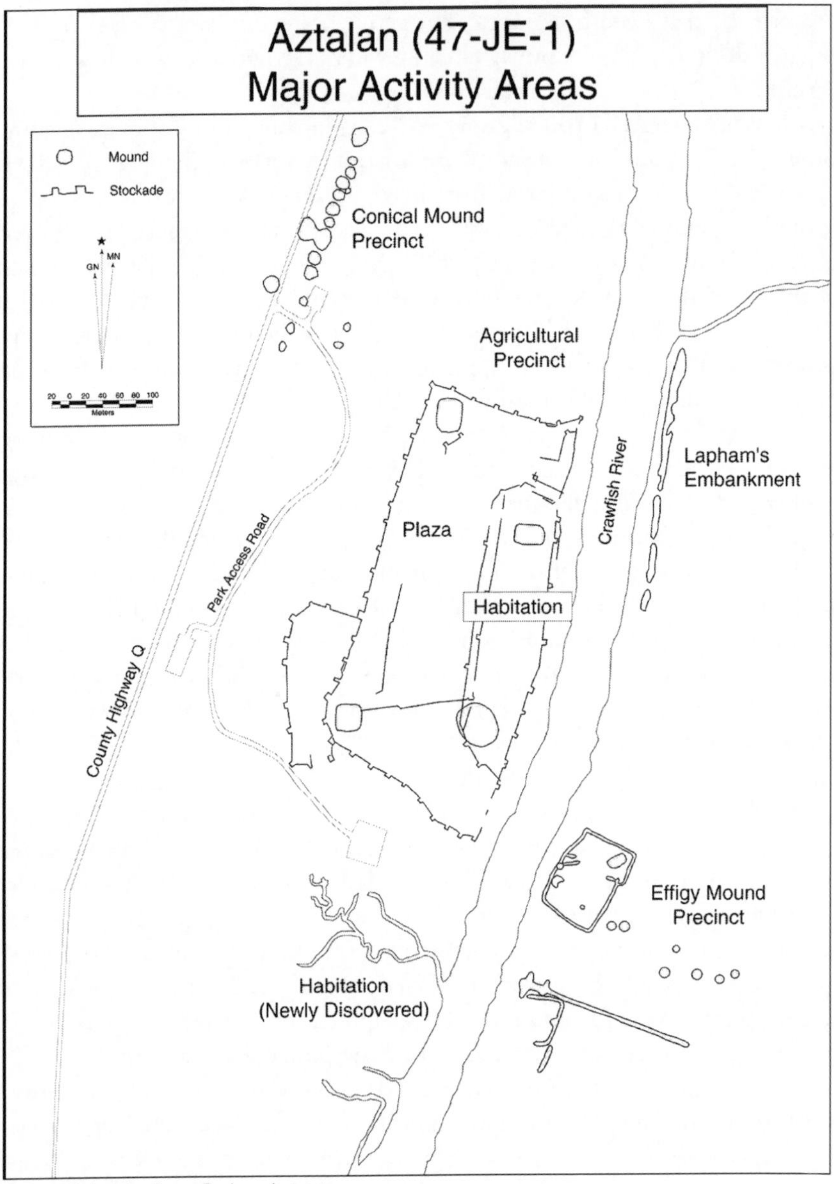
Aztalan (47-JE-1)
Major Activity Areas
Mound
Stockade
MN
GN
20 0 20 40 60 80 100
Meters
Conical Mound Precinct
Agricultural Precinct
Plaza
Habitation
Crawfish River
Lapham's Embankment
Park Access Road
County Highway Q
Effigy Mound Precinct
Habitation (Newly Discovered)

Figure C. Aztalan State Park and vicinity

of the walled community. On a high ridge overlooking these agricultural fields, the people of Aztalan constructed large round or conical mounds in several north-south trending lines. Many of the mounds marked the locations of huge wooden ceremonial posts that may have been used in agricultural rituals. Near the end of these ceremonial post mounds, was the mound grave of a mysterious woman dubbed by early researchers as the "princess" owing to several strands of shell beads in her tomb.

The Mississippians were not the stereotypically peaceful farmers of lore. Many Mississippian settlements were heavily fortified, and there is evidence of warfare and organized violence throughout Mississippian history. The Mississippians share this characteristic with other ancient (and not so ancient) civilizations throughout the world. Violence and warfare are major themes in Mississippian art and some have argued that human sacrifice accompanied certain rituals. The level of violence at Aztalan is much debated. The town was indeed strongly fortified and there is skeletal evidence of violence. Early twentieth-century researchers erroneously described the ancient people as cannibals who used their neighbors as food. The relationship between Aztalan and its neighbors is one of the important research questions being pursued by scholars using archaeological evidence from Aztalan and ancient village sites throughout the region. Indeed, while much has been learned about this spectacular site over the years, many great questions remain.

In this book, we present many interesting and provocative ideas about Aztalan and its origins and demise based on current evidence and thinking. We examine the culture that gave birth to the town and the dynamic cultural processes at work in the Upper Midwest at the time of its founding. We describe the site in the context of the customs and cosmology of the Mississippians and their allies, and discuss lifeways of the townspeople as reflected in the variety of artifacts recovered by archaeologists throughout the years. The book concludes with the story of the long and successful efforts to preserve the remains of the town as Wisconsin's premier archaeological site. We begin, however, with how archaeologists and other scholars have solved much of the mystery of Aztalan over a century and a half of research.

ONE

Solving the Mysteries

A young settler named Timothy Johnson reportedly first came upon the ruins of Aztalan in the summer of 1836. Hearing of the reports of an ancient walled city, Nathaniel Hyer traveled on horseback from the village of Milwaukee in 1836, and again in early 1837, to complete the first map of the site. He first sent a brief description to the Chicago American newspaper and on February 25, 1837, published a map and lengthier description in the Milwaukee Advertiser. It was Hyer who gave the site its name, relating it to the Aztecs and the observations of Prussian naturalist and scientific traveler, Alexander Von Humboldt:

> The accompanying cut, together with the above description is, intended to represent some of the "Ruins of an Ancient City;" which we have taken the liberty to call Aztalan, which name we find in the writings of Baron Humboldt, "From which it appears the people inhabiting the vale of Mexico, at the time the Spanish overrun that country, were called Azteeks or Aztekas and were as the Spanish history informs us usurpers from the North; from a country which they called Aztalan."[1]

Discovery of the mystifying ruins, widely reported in newspapers throughout the eastern United States, attracted both antiquarians and the curious to the banks of the Crawfish River. These visitors wrote about the ruins in national magazines, journals, and newspapers. The two driving questions throughout the nineteenth century became quite simply: What was Aztalan and who built it? Unfortunately, a great public interest in antiquities at the time led to a flood of relic hunters who damaged the mounds while digging for ancient and sellable treasures.

A small, but bustling, settler's village, also named Aztalan, grew at the north end of the ancient town further promoting the prominence of the site and access to it. Situated in the heart of farming country, the village sprang up at the crossroads of two old Indian trails which now served as important transportation routes for distribution of produce to various markets. Hyer himself became so enamored of the place that he and some relatives moved to the village, becoming prominent citizens. A larger town was platted around the pioneer village that would have infringed on the north end of the site. Fortunately for those who would later want to study and preserve the ancient town, the plan never came to fruition. As was the case with many doomed pioneer settlements, the railroads bypassed the new town and the town did not grow to fill the designs of its early developers.

In 1838, W.T. Sterling began the first recorded digging at the ancient Indian town. Sterling, an antiquarian with an interest in Midwestern earthworks, excavated through one of the high ruined walls encircling the site, and concluded that the walls were constructed of fire-hardened clay mortar, not brick as Hyer had reported in his newspaper accounts.[2] Sterling also dug into what he termed the "largest oval mound in the enclosure" where, under a clay layer, he and his helpers encountered ash and burned bundles of human bones that had been tied together. We do not know which mound he explored: one possibility is the large natural knoll in the southeast corner of the town where other surprising discoveries would be made in the next century.

MAPPING AZTALAN

Increase A. Lapham, widely considered Wisconsin's first scientist, made a detailed map of the site in the 1850s. A transplant from Ohio with a surveying background, Lapham's interest in Native American antiquities can be traced his discovery of effigy mounds while laying out streets in the new village of Milwaukee. In 1855, the results of Lapham's subsequent research appeared as *The Antiquities of Wisconsin,* a landmark publication that was the first book on Wisconsin archaeology.[3]

An accomplished surveyor and gifted cartographer, Lapham described many intriguing features that Hyer had overlooked (Figure 1.1a and b). Lapham's explorations further compounded the mysteries of Aztalan. Digging into conical mounds on a ridge overlooking the ruins, he found that they covered locations of large wooden posts rather than human burials. He excavated into the ruined walls of the site and, contrary to earlier diggers, concluded that they were made of earth. Although Lapham thought that most earthworks in the state could be attributed to indigenous Native Americans, he was also struck by the similarity of the large, flat-topped earthen mounds at Aztalan to the stone pyramids of Mexico. He offered the theory that Aztalan had been founded by pre-Columbian Mexican colonists and that it functioned as a ceremonial site rather than as a fort.

Despite some efforts to preserve the site, Aztalan was left in the late nineteenth century to relic hunters and generations of farmers who plowed

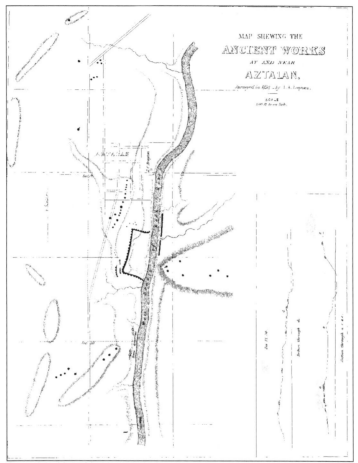

Figure 1.1a. Map of Aztalan area by Increase Lapham from his 1855 *Antiquities of Wisconsin*

down many of the distinctive features noted by Lapham and others. Farmers even tried to flatten the large platform mounds. When another ancient mound researcher, Theodore Lewis, visited in 1894 he found the site completely cultivated.[4] The loss of many visible features makes Lapham's maps and notes all the more valuable to modern researchers.

Like Lapham, Theodore Lewis was a surveyor with an eye for ancient cultural landscapes. Funded by a Minnesota businessman, Alfred Hill, he spent the years 1881–1894 mapping many thousands of mound sites throughout the Midwest—his maps becoming a treasure trove of information for modern researchers. Lewis and Hill hoped to compile information

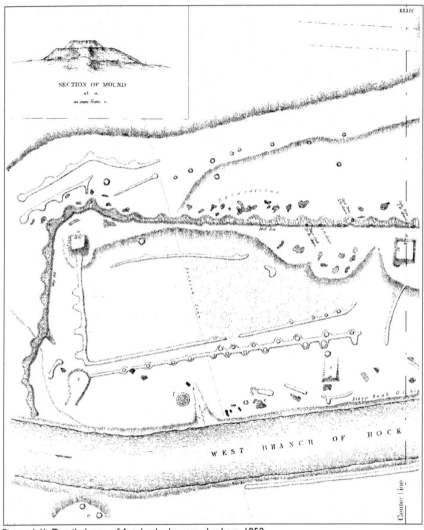

Figure 1.1b Detailed map of Aztalan by Increase Lapham, 1850

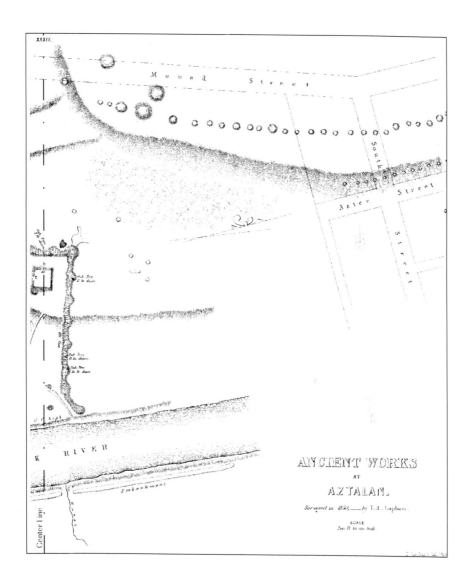

in the support of the contention, popular throughout the nineteenth century, that an ancient "lost race" constructed the many sophisticated earthworks, not the native Indians—hence their interest in mysterious Aztalan.

Lewis left no map of the main part of the site because so much had been obliterated. He did, however, map the opposite or east bank of the Crawfish River that added a piece to the Aztalan puzzle. Directly across from a major spring complex on the south side of Aztalan, Lewis found several earthen enclosures with some interior mounds and other earthworks that he called a "second fort". Later examination by Samuel Barrett of the Milwaukee Public Museum in 1920 identified one earthwork as a long-tailed effigy mound, the product of a local mound-building culture, quite different from the builders of Aztalan, and a way of life that disappeared as the town flourished (Figure 1.2).

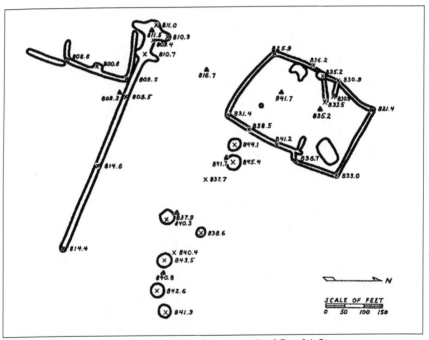

Figure 1.2. Barrett map of enclosure and mounds on east side of Crawfish River

TWENTIETH-CENTURY ARCHAEOLOGY

The turn of the century witnessed a revolution in approach to North American antiquities and ancient history. Largely stimulated by the

Smithsonian Institution's research to prove that Indians had created America's burial mounds and other earthworks, the field of North American archaeology emerged with a set of principles and techniques for excavating archaeological sites and new journals to disseminate research. At the same time, public interest in Native American artifacts and archaeological sites led to the formation of many amateur-based archaeological societies throughout the country. These amateurs did much of the work in the first part of the twentieth century since there were still few professionally trained archaeologists. The Wisconsin Archeological Society, formally chartered in 1906, was one of the earliest and most important of these amateur-based groups. Because of Aztalan's prominence and mystery, it would be of special interest to the Wisconsin Archeological Society and this group subsequently led efforts to document and preserve the site.

In 1907, George West wrote the first of many articles on Aztalan in the pages of the Wisconsin Archeological Society publication, *The Wisconsin Archeologist*. West, a Kenosha businessman, was an avid student of Native American cultures and a cofounder of the Wisconsin Archeological Society. In his article entitled "The Indian Authorship of Wisconsin Antiquities," he argued that the site was an ancient North American Indian settlement, and was not Mexican.[5] He pointed to the great similarity of the Aztalan platform mounds and walls to those described for southern North American Indian towns visited by the sixteenth-century Spanish conquistador Hernando De Soto and others.

BARRETT AND MILWAUKEE PUBLIC MUSEUM RESEARCH

Samuel A. Barrett was the first formally trained North American anthropologist to work in Wisconsin (Figure 1.3). He joined the staff of the Milwaukee Public Museum in 1909 and helped build it into a research institution of national renown. Under Barrett's direction, the museum staff spent two field seasons digging at Aztalan in 1919 and 1920, conducting the first professional and systematic archaeological excavations of any site in the state. He returned briefly for additional excavations in 1932.

Barrett's work resulted in the pioneering and classic book entitled *Ancient Aztalan* published in 1933.[6] His methods were crude by today's standards, but the book remains the most detailed and definitive work on Aztalan archaeology, and modern archaeologists consult it frequently for insights and information. The book's contents also provide a source of controversy.

Barrett's excavations focused mainly on the great ruined walls that once

Figure 1.3. Samuel A. Barrett of the Milwaukee Public Museum

surrounded and subdivided the site (Figures 1.4, 1.5). Digging through earth and fire-hardened clay, he found that the walls with evenly spaced mounds were not made of brick or earth, but were the collapsed remains of a huge wooden post stockade with large protruding bastions or watchtowers. The massive fortification had been coated with a thick plaster made of a mixture of clay and grass and it had burned sometime in the past. Excavating through thick piles of the former clay coating (called locally "Aztalan brick"), he found the large molds of the burned and rotted posts, positioned side by side, and in some cases, the bottoms of the posts themselves. Barrett determined that the wall was built using the wattle and daub technique—the people of Aztalan wove small branches through the vertical posts, and then plastered the wood wall with the clay mixture.

Figure 1.4. Photo of Barrett's excavations in the early 20th century (Barrett on left)

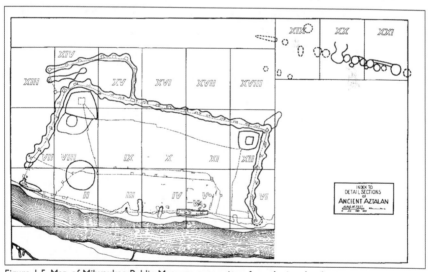

Figure 1.5. Map of Milwaukee Public Museum excavations from *Ancient Aztalan*

Sampling other portions of the site, Barrett discovered remains of small houses, also made by wattle and daub, as well as fire pits, storage and refuse pits, burials, many pieces of human bone, food remains, and many thousands of artifacts. He dug through the great southwest platform mound and found it had been built in stages, expanding the height and size of the structure. A low platform mound was constructed as the first stage, with a large ceremonial post at its center. During a later stage, a wooden pole enclosure rimmed the top of the mound that seemed to join two inner stockade walls that ran up the side of the mound. These inner stockade walls formed an entrance to what later archaeologists would call the plaza area.

Barrett confirmed Lapham's earlier discovery that the mounds on the ridge northwest of the town also covered locations of large ceremonial wooden posts. He thought it possible that the posts were erected during annual Green Corn ceremonies, a first fruits celebration held by more modern Indians throughout the southeastern part of the United States. These ceremonies included the raising of large ceremonial poles. However, digging at the north end of the mound line, Barrett discovered an elaborate human burial: a young woman who had been wrapped in thousands of shell beads. Barrett dubbed the woman "the princess" but the actual identity of this important person and the role she played in Aztalan society and history are part of the site's enduring mysteries. Human remains and burials continued to be excavated at archaeological sites like Aztalan through much of the twentieth century, although many Native Americans considered this desecration. Now, however, Wisconsin state law provides protection for all human burial places, and archaeologists and others are much more sensitive to Native American concerns. For many years the Milwaukee Public Museum featured a "princess" burial exhibit until growing sensitivity and respect for Native Americans forced its removal.

Confirming West's interpretation, Barrett found no evidence of Aztecs or other Mexican colonists. Instead, from physical features, pottery, and other artifacts, Barrett saw that Aztalan was similar to Cahokia and many other sites in the American Southeast, sites that had been recently defined by the new North American archaeologists as part of the Mississippian culture. Attesting to Barrett's sharp archaeological instincts, he correctly surmised that the site of Aztalan was occupied at about AD 1200.

Barrett also concluded that *two* different Indian peoples lived at the site at the same time, the Mississippians with their distinctive pottery and platform mound architecture, and a group of Woodland people, indigenous to the Upper Midwest, with a very different ceramic tradition. Some of the latter were the builders of Wisconsin's ubiquitous effigy mounds.

Barrett's most startling conclusion was that the people of Aztalan practiced true *cannibalism,* consuming human flesh and bone marrow as a source of food. He contrasted this with the practice of ritual cannibalism found in ancient cultures throughout the world. Barrett based this extraordinary claim on his discovery of many hundreds of butchered, broken, and burned human bones in refuse areas; severed limbs in fire pits; and discarded skulls, including one that clearly had been cut from the torso. Much of this evidence came from the area near a large natural knoll at the southeast corner of the town. While modern studies refute Barrett's conclusion that the people of Aztalan relied on human beings for food, this conclusion remained part of the official interpretation for many years because the behavior represented by the remains was so different from anything archaeologists had seen to date.

RECONSTRUCTION: THE WISCONSIN ARCHAEOLOGICAL SURVEY EXCAVATIONS

Barrett's publication greatly accelerated public and professional cries to preserve the remarkable site from continued farming. The Wisconsin Archeological Society bought a small part of the site in 1928 but it was not until after the Great Depression and World War II that the state of Wisconsin itself could respond to the call. In 1948, the Department of Conservation (now the Department of Natural Resources) acquired the entire site with the intent to develop a state park.

By that time, professional archaeology had grown dramatically due to the proliferation of programs at universities and museums after the war. In 1948, professionals working in the state formed the Wisconsin Archeological Survey to help coordinate state research. Both the acquisition of the site and the presence of an organized professional work force generated a dramatic new phase of archaeological research that lasted into the 1960s. A cadre of students working on degrees at the University of Wisconsin–Madison, the first group of professionally trained Wisconsin archaeologists, conducted much of the research. These researchers used new scientific techniques and procedures and applied them in their work. Among these was radiocarbon dating which firmly established that Aztalan flourished between AD 900 and 1250, after which time it was abandoned.

Supported by the Department of Conservation, archaeological work between 1949 and 1952 acquired new information about the site and worked to reconstruct portions of the site for public viewing in the new state park. Among those leading field parties were David Baerreis and Robert Maher of the University of Wisconsin–Madison, Chandler Rowe of Lawrence College, and Moreau Maxwell of Beloit College. Their results were reported in "Aztalan: Exploration and Reconstruction," published in *The Wisconsin Archeologist* in 1958.[7] The work, which included a long trench excavated through the site by heavy machinery, added much toward understanding the architectural and cultural variation across the site, and the function of the platform mound at the northwest corner of the town.

The work exposed remnants of more small houses of different styles in the innermost stockade near the river. These remnants consisted of small circular post impressions or molds that outlined the house shape. Like the walls, one house was burned and filled with charred debris. To the south of the town, the archaeologists found the remains of an oval structure bisected by a simple log wall or stockade. This suggests either the presence of a former village or perhaps the existence of buildings outside of the town walls.

Archaeologists defined new types of Woodland pottery that were not Mississippian. Among these is a style now known as Aztalan Collared, a pottery type that clearly evolved from earlier styles found in the Upper Midwest. Another is Point Sauble Collared made by Woodland peoples throughout eastern Wisconsin. These different pottery-making traditions, along with different styles of houses, are evidence of the cosmopolitan nature of the town.

Archaeologists also examined the great southwest platform mound, which had suffered greatly by years of plowing. They confirmed that it was built in stages and that the people of Aztalan built a large enclosure on top of the mound during a later stage of construction. They also found that the mound had been faced with a mantle of light-colored clay that would have provided a visually impressive appearance. These features are similar to what has been found at other Mississippian sites, including Cahokia. At many Mississippian sites, enclosures surrounded the houses of the important families. Historical documents from the American Southeast describe chiefs or town rulers living on large platform mounds and that these chiefly residential mounds were frequently distinguished by mantles of light-colored soil.

Excavation of the northwest platform mound at Aztalan revealed a different function altogether. Like the great southwest mound, this mound was built in stages, three to be exact. On the top of the second building stage, and covered by the third-stage addition, Chandler Rowe discovered a small burned wattle and daub structure measuring twelve feet by five feet containing the skeletal remains of eleven people.[8] Rowe called the structure a crematorium but it is more properly viewed as the burned remains of a charnel house, a mortuary building similar to a mausoleum commonly found on platform mounds in later southern Mississippian towns. As described by early explorers, these special buildings contained the corpses of important Mississippian individuals and their relatives. The northwest mound at Aztalan appears to have been the mortuary mound for the elite people of the town. Unfortunately, over a century of plowing obliterated the top of the mound, so it is impossible to say whether or not a similar structure existed on the third and final stage of construction.

Weighing in on the cannibalism hypothesis, Paul Parmalee, a noted expert on animal food remains, then at the Illinois State Museum, analyzed bone found by Barrett and the Wisconsin Archeological Survey excavations.[9] He concluded that although there was intriguing evidence that some human bone had been processed like animal bone, cracked and split open for nutritious marrow, for example, the town's protein came mainly from deer, fish, birds, clams, and other local animal life.

WHERE THE PEOPLE LIVED AND THEIR SACRED FIRE: WISCONSIN HISTORICAL SOCIETY EXCAVATIONS

Archaeological work resumed at the site in the 1960s under the direction of state archaeologist Joan Freeman of the Wisconsin Historical Society, a University of Wisconsin–Madison graduate who had participated in earlier work.[10] Although some sections of previously excavated walls were examined, a major part of Freeman's work concentrated on the residential area along the river, defining many more small houses of various styles (Figures 1.6a, b, and c). At the north end of this zone, the team excavated the north-

Figure 1.6a. Wisconsin Archeological Survey excavation showing interior stockade line and bastion (foreground)

Figure 1.6b. Joan Freeman of the Wisconsin Historical Society oversees bulldozer removal of plowed and disturbed layer of earth from site.

Figure 1.6c. Wisconsin Historical Society hand-excavated area showing remnants of structures and pits

east platform mound first examined by Barrett. They discovered that it supported yet another type of common Mississippian structure: a temple for the sacred fire. Unlike the other two platform mounds, this one was constructed in a single stage. However, this mound covered the remains of an open-walled structure made of upright poles that had been built into the original land surface. After construction of the mound, the people of Aztalan erected an identical structure on top of the mound; this structure contained fire pits filled with layers of charcoal and white sand. Aztalan archaeologists believe that these structures represent public buildings where religious specialists maintained a sacred fire, a custom found throughout the Mississippian world. Indeed, white sand is a purifying agent in the beliefs of many Native American cultures. Periodically, the fires would have been extinguished and rekindled in world renewal ceremonies.

MODERN RESEARCH

In the mid 1970s, the University of Wisconsin–Milwaukee developed a regional program called the Southeastern Wisconsin Archaeological Project under the direction of Lynne Goldstein. Building on a small previous survey of the countryside surrounding Aztalan by Loyola University,[11] the program was the first to systematically examine the area around Aztalan and analyze the ancient town in its broader context. Funded in part by federal historic preservation grants administered by the Wisconsin Historical Society, University of Wisconsin–Milwaukee archaeologists examined many thousands of acres in the Crawfish River region and located over four hundred and fifty ancient Indian sites. But the archaeologists found no other site like Aztalan and only a few that showed Mississippian influence.[12] The study reaffirmed the uniqueness of Aztalan.

The project moved to Aztalan itself in 1984 when University of Wisconsin–Milwaukee archaeologists dug into an area most likely to provide a history of the site's occupation—a large garbage accumulation, also called a midden, that had been noted by Barrett and other early investigators along the river. Carefully excavating and sifting eight feet down into this long-ago dump, the archaeologists found neat layers of deposits spanning hundreds of years (Figure 1.7). University of Wisconsin–Milwaukee archaeologist John Richards, who analyzed the contents, found that each layer told a different story, and together the information traced the history of the town from a small Woodland farming village to the sudden appearance of the Mississippians with their distinctive architecture and culture.[13] The layers of dirt included soil eroded off the town and fields as a result of massive landscape modifications such as the creation of the central plaza, as well as the

Figure 1.7. Profile through garbage midden along the Crawfish River from University of Wisconsin–Milwaukee excavations

more recent farming practices. Work in the formerly enclosed middle zone of the town, thought to have been the plaza, led to the discovery of houses that appear to date to a time before the creation of the plaza, as well as large deep pits that had been used for communal feasts and storage of ritual items when the town flourished.

In 1996, Goldstein joined the faculty of Michigan State University, bringing students of that university to study different aspects of the site (Figure 1.8). Among the new discoveries was that the plaza area just south of the northwest platform mound, the area containing the deep storage pits, was a highly modified land surface virtually sculpted into a tiered or terraced surface.[14] The nature of this modification is the subject of ongoing research: in historic times Mississippians put much effort in the creation and maintenance of public plazas used for ceremonies, dances, feasts, and ritual games. Goldstein coined the term "sculptuary" for this sculpted landscape and believes that it is also related to elaborate mortuary rituals.

Michigan State University archaeological work also has extended to areas outside of the town itself. Excavations have been conducted to search for the agricultural fields to the north of the stockade and in an area to the south where Late Woodland and Mississippian features have been discovered, undisturbed by modern agricultural practices. On the east side of the Crawfish River, opposite of the town, work focused around a smaller enclo-

Figure 1.8. University of Wisconsin–Milwaukee excavations in progress

sure and mounds described by Lewis and Barrett, as well as surrounding lands where earlier surveys identified some ancient artifacts and features. Artifacts recovered on this side of the river are mainly Late Woodland, although there is also evidence of limited use by Mississippians. A long embankment along the river mapped by Lapham appears to be of human construction, but its purpose is unknown. The nature of the small enclosure itself, which is not visible today, remains a mystery. Goldstein believes it may have been remnants of effigy mounds.

A major and important component of modern archaeological work has involved bringing together the results and locations of all of the previous archaeological work, extending back into the nineteenth century, into a single database that can produce accurate maps of the site. Goldstein and Michigan State University staff developed a computer Geographic Information System (GIS) that now allows researchers and planners to more easily address many different questions about Aztalan research.

Other new technologies also are aiding Aztalan research. Remote sensing equipment, which measures below-surface soil differences by radar or electromagnetic signals, allows for the comparatively rapid location of former walls, pits, and other disturbances, eliminating the need for massive exploratory excavations (Figures 1.9a and b). In 2003, for example, electro-

Figures 1.9a and b. Woody Wallace, of Earth Information Technology, pulls a remote sensing device mounted on a sled behind an ATV to detect below ground disturbances. The apparatus is linked to satellite Global Positioning System to track locations.

magnetic conductivity remote sensing by the Wisconsin Historical Society's Office of the State Archaeologist and Earth Information Technology Inc. revealed that some belowground features still exist in the area of the mysterious, walled southwest enclosure in the southwest corner of the town. These appear to include remnants of some features mapped by Lapham in the 1850s before the aboveground evidence disappeared under the plow. University of Wisconsin–Milwaukee archaeologists have also experimented with electromagnetic techniques along with other remote sensing techniques called ground penetrating radar and soil resistivity, in other areas of the site.[15] They located what may be structures, palisade lines, and even previously excavated areas.

FUTURE RESEARCH

Over the years, archaeological research at Aztalan has turned our understanding of the site from a fortress built by a mysterious race to an ancient Indian ceremonial town with origins in the mighty Mississippian civilization that once flourished in the Midwest and across the southeastern United States. Limited research continues at the site defining new areas of interest and clarifying areas identified by previous archaeologists. Archaeologists are now aided by new technology, such as remote sensing and computer mapping to analyze the site. Further, scholars from many institutions are poring over the thousands of artifacts and mountains of data collected by previous researchers over nearly a century of excavations, offering new and frequently surprising insights on this remarkable site. Archaeological studies elsewhere in the state and the country also continue to aid in our understanding of Aztalan. The archaeological work, combined with a rich historical record describing customs of later platform mound-building societies in North America, sheds much light on the remarkable people that built Aztalan. Therefore, we now turn to the great Mississippian civilization and its spectacular metropolis, Cahokia—the probable origin place of many of Aztalan's people.

TWO

The People of the Sun

Although people of two different Indian cultures lived there, Aztalan was a classic Mississippian town in virtually all respects. In order to understand its layout, the beliefs and lifeways of its people, and even explanations for its existence in Wisconsin, we now examine the remarkable civilization that gave it birth and molded its history.

ORIGINS

In at least one sense, Lapham and other nineteenth-century thinkers may not have been too terribly wrong about a Mexican connection for sites like Aztalan. The roots of the Mississippian civilization can in fact be traced to Mexico in the form of a crop called *zea mays*, better known as corn. Developed from a wild grass called *teosinte*, it was first domesticated in central Mexico over four thousand years ago. Over the next several thousand years, seeds from this crop and undoubtedly a complex of other cultural ideas and innovations spread northward up the Mississippi River into mid-continental North America.

The spread of corn agriculture into North America is not surprising. For thousands of years there had been trade and interaction between peoples of Mesoamerica. Some scholars even point to the platform mounds and similarities in mythology to argue that cultural contact with Mexico, specifically the Toltecs, stimulated Mississippian development. But so far there is no evidence of direct contact.

Whatever the pathway, an agricultural revolution occurred once corn was introduced into the vast and fertile bottomlands of the Mississippi River near the modern-day city of St. Louis. After AD 800, here, in what is called the American Bottom, the diverse indigenous Woodland peoples developed agricultural communities that rapidly evolved into Cahokia, an American Indian ceremonial city with vast influence.[1]

CAHOKIA

The Indian city of Cahokia was without doubt the most remarkable place in pre-Columbian North America (Figure 2.1). Covering over five square miles of Mississippi River floodplain, an estimated 10,000–15,000 people lived here at AD 1150.

Cahokia was a highly organized society. At the center of the diamond-shaped metropolis was a great plaza ringed by large earthen platform mounds, other mounds, and the houses of important families. A massive two-mile-long stockade walled off this urban center from the rest of the city. Like some other Mississippian communities, the mounds and other principal features were oriented on a north-south axis, the cardinal directions were very important in Mississippian beliefs and ritual. At the north end of this urban center is Monks Mound, the largest earthen construction in North America. Covering sixteen acres and rising one hundred feet above the plaza, the four-stepped mound is believed to have supported the residence of great paramount chiefs—the lords of the Mississippian civilization.

Figure 2.1. The Mississippian City of Cahokia

South of the plaza lies a smaller but remarkable tomb complex used for about a hundred years that included the graves of the Mississippian elite. Known today as Mound 72, it provides an extraordinary insight into the complexity of Cahokia and Mississippian society as a whole.[2] The main mound itself was built over 232 human burials that had been laid on the surface of the ground as well as interred in three smaller mounds. The complex contained thousands of grave objects, many of them made from rare and exotic materials sometimes imported from great distances such as copper, mica, stone for arrow points, red pipestone, and conch or whelk shell from the Atlantic Ocean or Gulf of Mexico.

In one of the interior mounds covered by Mound 72, an extremely important man was laid to rest on a bed of twenty thousand shell beads, arranged in the shape of a hawk or most probably a falcon—a recurring motif in Mississippian art. Made from seashells imported from the Gulf of Mexico, the beads attest to the status of the man. Additional burials surrounded the grave. Four skeletons of men lacked heads and hands. Mortuary objects in the vicinity included beautifully chipped arrows of various colored stones, copper, and other luxurious items.

One large grave pit in Mound 72 contained the remains of fifty-three young women neatly laid out in rows. In another, less orderly pit, men and women appear to have been killed by arrows and other means. Above this pit was another series of burials, some on wooden litters, a symbol of high status in Mississippian society (Figure 2.2). Skeletal analysis suggests that some of the people may have come from outside of Cahokia proper.[3]

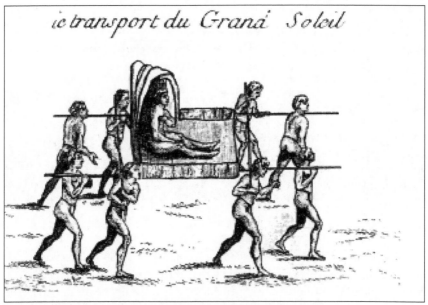

Figure 2.2. Mississippian nobles were carried on litters. This early French drawing from Le Page Du Pratz (1758) shows the "Great Sun" of the Natchez. Mound 72 at Cahokia contained many burials of people with litters, suggesting high status.

Some archaeologists believe that many of these burials were human sacrifices. University of Wisconsin–Milwaukee professor emeritus Melvin Fowler, who supervised much of the excavation of Mound 72, believes that many of the people interred in the mound were sacrificed during the funeral rituals for dignitaries like the beaded bird man and those on the litters.[4] Indeed, later Mississippians customarily killed family members and retainers during the funeral rites for chiefs or important people. In 1728, a French visitor to the Natchez in the southeastern United States witnessed the ritual strangulation of young women during the funeral procession of Tattooed Serpent, brother of the Great Sun.[5]

However, other analyses by Goldstein and James Brown, a Mississippian expert at Northwestern University, indicate that many of the burials in Mound 72 were the result of "secondary burial," a custom practiced by some Native American societies from ancient times into the historic period, and particularly well documented for the Mississippians.[6] This custom involved saving and processing the corpses and bones of some people for later burial during special ritual occasions and in special places that represented a common social identity or ancestry for those interred. In *Ancient Cahokia and the Mississippians,* Timothy Pauketat argues that Mound 72 reflects both the interment of important individuals and "periodic commemorations possibly tied to a ritual calendar" when sacrifices were made and the dead were brought to the place as bones or in various stages of decay.[7] Whatever the case, the complexity of Cahokia society is obviously reflected in the complexity of Mound 72.

Dense residential districts ringed the Cahokia center along with other ceremonial places. Houses were single-family wattle and daub structures plastered with clay on the outside for weatherproofing. In some cases, platform mounds elevated the houses above the ground. These may have been the residences of clan chiefs or other important people. Ceremonial areas included a large circle of posts called a "woodhenge" that is believed to have been a solar calendar for the scheduling of great religious events based on the summer and winter solstices. The city itself was surrounded by thousands of acres of cornfields, smaller ceremonial centers, villages, and farming hamlets.

THE MISSISSIPPIAN REGION

Just how big a region Cahokia directly controlled is unknown. However, from the American Bottom, the new Mississippian lifestyle spread rapidly over the Mississippi River drainage to the Gulf of Mexico to the south, the Atlantic Coast to the east, the Great Plains to the west, and as far north as the Great Lakes (Figure 2.3). It changed local cultural practices and unified

Figure 2.3. The Mississippian region eventually extended over much of eastern North America and included many major towns and sites.

much of eastern North America with common religious ideas, social structures, and monumental architecture.

Long after the perplexing demise of Cahokia itself, the Mississippian culture flourished in the southeastern United States until the entrance of the Europeans. Spanish and French explorers described the well-organized Mississippian towns with characteristic platform mounds, and also recorded their beliefs and customs. Some of the bearers of Mississippian culture we now know as the Creek, Natchez, Chickasaw, Choctaw, Cherokee, Alabama, and Caddo.

Later Mississippian towns were not as large as Cahokia but shared similar designs including town centers with large plazas and earthen platform mounds that supported chiefly dwellings and other important structures, all surrounded by residential areas.[8] Heavy fortifications, with carefully controlled and guarded access points, enclosed the typical town. Many Mississippian societies were already changing before European contact but they were also greatly affected by the arrival of the Europeans and the introduction of European infectious diseases, warfare, and dislocation of people.

BELIEFS AND COSMOLOGY

The Mississippians did not utilize a written language but they left behind remarkable and detailed representations of their beliefs in the form of large stone figurines, effigy smoking pipes, stone tablets, shell engravings, ceramic designs, and even drawings on the walls of ritual caves. This iconography, along with firsthand accounts by European explorers and more recent anthropological and historical research among the descendents of Mississippian peoples, provide a rich picture of religious beliefs and themes.

The Mississippian belief system elaborated and formalized concepts that had great antiquity in North America and are shared by many Native American people to this very day. Like many of the world's belief systems and religions, the underlying structure was dualistic, dividing the real and supernatural worlds into upper and lower levels with the earth and humans in between. The upper world was orderly while the lower world was more chaotic. The purpose of many ceremonies was to maintain or restore balance between the worlds, sometimes by ritually recreating the cosmos.

Among Native Americans, the upper world is represented and personified by celestial bodies, the sun, moon, and stars, as well as birds of the air, both real and supernatural. One common inhabitant of the upper world among Native Americans is the thunderbird, perceived as an eagle-like spirit that causes thunder and lightning. Among the Mississippians, the falcon was especially revered. The lower world is subdivided into earth and water realms, including a watery and menacing underworld filled with snakes, serpents, and monsters. This underlying bird and serpent dichotomy was shared with cultures of Mesoamerica leading some to suggest a common origin in the mists of antiquity.[9]

Rattlesnakes also were important to Mississippians, being both feared and admired. In some Native American stories, the rattlesnake saves humans from disease, and thus is viewed as a shield against sickness. One stone effigy pipe found at Cahokia appears to be a kneeling shaman or priest holding a gourd rattle with a rattlesnake or rattlesnake skin around his neck.[10] In Native American societies, shamans are medicine men who draw upon special powers to alleviate sickness and disease. They are often part of formal medicine societies from which they learn the necessary medicines and rituals.

The underlying dualism of the Mississippian world is clearly expressed at Mound 72. Here, the man on the beaded bird platform was interred above another burial, one face down, and oriented in the opposite direction. Melvin Fowler suggests the birdman was a sky world chief while the opposing burial below was the chief of the earth or lower world.[11]

As noted, the cardinal directions also were important to the Mississippians, subdividing the cosmos into quadrants. Cahokia itself was laid out on a north-south, east-west axis that subdivided the town into four quadrants, apparently representing the four corners of the world. In Mississippian and other Native American cultures, the east-west axis traces the daily passage of the sun itself, from birth to death.

Much Mississippian imagery relates to these themes. The solar deity is represented by a cross and circle, the cross signifying the four cardinal directions. Birds, especially falcons, are common representations, many times in the form of men dressed as these birds of prey (Figure 2.4). The falcon is the symbol of warriors and warfare. The watery underworld includes water-related beings known as water spirits or underground water panthers in later Indian

Figure 2.4. Drawing of Bird-dancer inscribed on a conch shell from the Spiro Site in Oklahoma (AD 1200–1600)

cultures. Among the Cherokee, the underwater monster is called *Uktena* and is viewed as a winged creature with antlers and a scaly body.

One culture hero in Mississippian mythology has received much attention due to the discoveries of painted images in several one-thousand-year-old ritual caves in Wisconsin and Missouri. This is the warrior Red Horn, also known as "He Who Wears Human Heads as Earrings." Much is known about this legendary figure because his exploits were still recounted in modern times by the related Siouan-speaking people indigeneous to the Upper Midwest—the Ho-Chunk (or Winnebago) and Ioway.[12] The distant ancestors of these people probably had direct contact with the Mississippians, sharing many cultural ideas, including the Red Horn stories.

University of Illinois at Chicago professor emeritus Robert L. Hall, an expert on Native American belief systems, associates the small shell or copper human head earrings found at Mississippian sites with the Red Horn legend.[13] These artifacts, called long-nosed god maskettes, have been found in Illinois, Iowa, Missouri, and Wisconsin, including Aztalan. Male figures wearing these earrings, or associated with similar objects, also appear on shell engravings, a stone pipe from Spiro, Oklahoma, and in Mississippian-style cave art in Missouri and Wisconsin (Figure 2.5). Rock wall paintings at

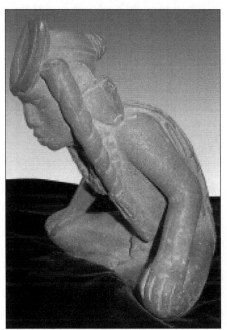

Figure 2.5. The Resting Warrior or "Big Boy" Figurine from the Spiro Site, Oklahoma. Note human head earrings.

the Gottschall Rockshelter in Wisconsin appear to depict a recorded story about Red Horn or his son battling giants with the help of a thunderbird and a turtle.[14] In another recorded story, Red Horn is killed but magically brought back to life, becoming a symbol for rebirth.

In Mississippian art, warriors are sometimes depicted wearing human head earrings, perhaps to become Red Horn with his indestructibility. Robert Hall also believes that the long-nosed god maskettes were used to identify individuals representing Red Horn and his sons in adoption ceremonies that created kinship relationships with allies and trading partners. He draws an analogy with the Calumet ceremony conducted between different tribes of the Upper Midwest and Great Plains in historic times. Here, trading relationships were established by adopting the trade partner in a kinship group, the partner now replacing a specific deceased kin. Among the ceremonies was the ritual smoking of the special calumet pipe.

Mississippian life revolved around many ceremonies and rituals that guided life and death. Being an agricultural society, it is not surprising that many rituals and much symbolism related to fertility. One of the most important annual ceremonies was the mid-summer Green Corn ceremony also called the Busk.[15] This consisted of several days of feasting, dancing, and ritual to celebrate the ripening of the first corn. The celebration took place

Figures 2.6a and b. Birger Figurine from the BBB Motor Site in Illinois (front and back)

around a special pole put up for the occasion and also involved the rekindling of a sacred fire, symbolic of rebirth of the world.

Fertility is a major Mississippian artistic theme. Among the rare and beautiful statuettes is the famous Birger Figurine, found at a site near Cahokia, and that has clear fertility symbolism.[16] A woman is depicted hoeing the back of a serpent with a panther-like face and gourds growing from its body (Figures 2.6a and b). In the Mississippian belief system, serpents and other watery underworld creatures, both natural and supernatural, are associated with rain, water, and fertility, among other things.

SOCIAL AND POLITICAL SYSTEM

Cahokia and Mississippian society was so vast and complex that some scholars once believed that it formed the first state or nation—an Indian empire—north of Mesoamerica. However, most now agree that Mississippian societies were *chiefdoms,* social and political systems that are hierarchical in form but are based on kinship. The Mississippian communities in the American Southeast shared a common culture but were not politically unified. Rival chiefdoms developed, frequently at war with one another.

Like other Native American societies, kinship determined social relations. Who you were in Mississippian society was defined by membership in a clan traced through the female line—a person belonged to his or her mother's clan. In most Native Americans societies, clans occupy similar social positions although clans may have different responsibilities. Among the Ho-Chunk or Winnebago of Wisconsin, for example, the members of the Thunderbird Clan supply civil chiefs, the Bear Clan is responsible for public order, and the Water Spirit Clan deals with water issues.[17] In the past, the Ho-Chunk also had a Warrior Clan.

In Mississippian society, the clans may have had different responsibilities. Further, the clans were ranked in importance with those at the top enjoying greater prestige and status. Among the Natchez, and some others, the highest-ranking clan was called the Sun clan.[18] Natchez rulers came from this clan through the female line and were believed to be brothers of the sun. One chiefly symbol was the cross and circle enclosed by a litter; litter transport was reserved for leaders. Other levels of rank in Mississippian society were priestly advisors who formed an elite group, community leaders, warriors, and commoners who worked the fields and produced goods. War captives were used very much like slaves. However, the various levels of Mississippian society were fluid, and therefore were not closed social and economic classes. In fact, it would appear that people were obligated to marry outside of their own clan.

THE MATERIAL WORLD

Agriculture formed the base of the Mississippian economy. Besides corn, grown in great quantities, the Mississippian farmers raised squash, pumpkins, and sunflowers. They also fished, hunted game (particularly deer), and gathered berries and nuts. Large animals like deer not only provided meat but also skins needed for clothing, blankets, moccasins, and other material needs. In chiefdoms, political and religious leaders redistributed food and other goods to the general population during ceremonies, rituals, and feasts.

Mississippians used natural materials gathered from around their communities and acquired through trade from other regions. They used tree saplings to form the superstructure of houses and waterproofed the walls with layers of clay. Prairie grass provided thatching for roofs. They made garments from deer hides as well as from fabrics hand spun from animal fur and plant fibers like dogbane and milkweed.[19]

Wood, stone, animal bone, and shell supplied raw material for tools. Some tools were so beautifully made that full-time craftsman or specialists must have done the work. The finely made Mississippian arrowheads are distinctive in the use of small notches for hafting. Of particular importance were the many types of chert, a flint-like stone that could be chipped into knives, scrapers, arrowheads, and hoes. For example, Mississippians obtained a special chert for hoe manufacture, called Mill Creek, from quarries in southern Illinois. The Mississippians also used granite for axes and other stones for grinding vegetable food.

While chert, an easily chipped silica stone, and other rock usually could be found locally, the Mississippians at Cahokia sometimes acquired specially colored or otherwise symbolically important stone from other places. Wisconsin is represented by Hixton Silicified Sandstone, a golden or sun-colored rock found only in the west-central part of the state. A cache of Hixton arrowheads was found near the Mound 72 beaded birdman burial, along with arrowheads representing bundles of once complete arrows, from other regions.

The Mississippians traded for many other exotic and highly prized objects that were used to reinforce the status of leaders. Whelk and other seashells, for example, were imported from the Gulf of Mexico and made into pendants, beads, and ornaments only used by the elite. Copper was obtained from northern Michigan. Lead for white paint, including body paint, came from Missouri and Wisconsin.

Figure 2.7. Interlocking Scroll motif on Ramey vessel from Aztalan

Mississippians made a vast array of pottery forms for food preparation, storage, and special purposes. These forms included pans, bowls, plates, jars, beakers, and bottles. Some of the most beautiful ceramics were used in rituals and ceremonies. These included shell cups, dipping gourds, and ceramic vessels known as Ramey Incised. Ramey vessels are exquisitely made jars, often colored black, and often bearing a distinctive interlocking scroll motif that is believed to be symbolic of fertility and life regeneration (Figure 2.7).[20] Observers of the Green Corn ceremony in more recent times stated that the occasion required the manufacture of special ceramic vessels for special cleansing medicines.[21] Ramey jars may have been such special vessels used by the ancient Mississippians.

PHYSICAL APPEARANCE

The Mississippians left behind a remarkable record of their personal appearance in the depictions of themselves in many art media. Using natural pigments, they painted and tattooed their faces and bodies in a variety of patterns. The main colors were red, yellow, white, and black. Hair was often put into a thick braid, wound around their head or worn as a bun. Men, especially warriors, shaved or plucked hair from the sides of their heads and braided the tops into long forelocks. Both men and women wore wrap-around kilts spun from animal hair and plant fibers. The ceremonial garb of chiefs and other notables included feathered headdresses; earspools made from copper, stone, and shell; and capes of shell beads and feathers (Figure 2.8).[22]

Figure 2.8. Mississippian elite people

CHUNKEY: AN INDIAN NATIONAL PASTIME

The Mississippians played a variety of games, but none as important as one involving spear-throwing skills, called chunkey or chunky in more recent times. So widespread and popular was the game that it has been called the Mississippian "national pastime."[23] Chunkey, played on specially prepared playing fields, was a contest between players who threw spears at a small, rolling stone disk, generally made of granite (Figure 2.9). The object of the game was to come closest to where the stone stopped rolling. The wheel-like chunkey stones, found at many Mississippian sites including Aztalan, are concave and sometimes decorated with symbols that called for supernatural assistance.

Figure 2.9. Chunkey game as played by the Mandan

The game began appearing in settlements in the American Bottom just prior to the rise of Cahokia. In later times the game seems to have been restricted to Mississippian ceremonial centers.[24] Like the more lethal ball games of Mesoamerica in which participants were occasionally sacrificed, chunkey played an important social and religious role and therefore was played quite seriously. Chunkey contests were public spectacles: in more recent times, onlookers bet heavily on the matches that often lasted all day. A large cache of chunkey stones found buried with the beaded birdman in Mound 72 at Cahokia reflects the great prestige associated with the game.

Chunkey players themselves were also the subject of Mississippian art. One Mississippian stone figure, thought to have been found at Cahokia, is of a player holding chunkey stones and two chunkey spears. He is naked but for earspools and a single bead necklace. In contrast, a marine shell found in Missouri depicts a chunkey player as an elaborately dressed warrior-chieftain.

FALCON-WARRIORS

Warfare and violence seem to have been a part of Mississippian life from the beginning and increasingly so as time went on. Settlements were heavily fortified and warfare was a major theme of Mississippian art. Images in many media feature warriors dancing with stylized war clubs and the severed heads of enemies. One stone figurine is of a warrior in the act of decapitating a dead enemy (Figure 2.10). Other figures depict war captives and in this light, some have suggested that some of the ritual sacrifices in Mound 72 may have been war captives.

Figure 2.10. Reconstructed effigy pipe bowl from the Spiro Site, Oklahoma (AD 1200–1600) depicting Mississippian warrior decapitating an enemy

Warriors dressed and painted or tattooed themselves as falcons, complete with the forked eye pattern and spotted breast found on the bird itself. The falcon became a war symbol because of its swiftness and aggressiveness. Images of warriors, including art on the walls of ritual caves, depict warriors throughout the Mississippian region in similar garb and body treatment, complete with thick, thatched chest armor. This suggests the presence of an organized warrior society, recruited from the populace as a whole or from specific clans.

DEATH AND BURIAL

The Mississippians practiced an array of funerary and mortuary customs that reflect varying status in life. At the lower rungs of society, many people were buried in small family or clan cemeteries near their homes. The bodies of individuals from high-ranking clans or kinship groups close to the chiefs went through a more complex death ritual. They were first placed in temporary charnel houses or mortuary temples atop platform mounds. Stone, clay, or wood images depicting the people themselves, ancestors, or culture heroes adorned the charnel house interior and priests cared for the bones.[25] Periodically, the charnel houses were burned or the bones removed to be buried or stored elsewhere, sometimes in conjunction with great events, such as the death of a chief.

Prior to final burial, the bones were often bundled and tied together. If decay had not taken place completely, the body was cut apart and the bones separated and carefully cleaned. In bundling and bone reburial ceremonies, attention focused mainly on certain anatomical parts—skulls, hands, and long bones—as though these were the essence of the individual. Remaining bones were often discarded. The skulls of honored ancestors may have been retained by relatives for veneration after burial of the other body parts. The mortuary customs were often complex and seemed to vary according to circumstances and social situations, but a considerable amount of handling and processing of human remains was part of Mississippian ritual before the bones were finally laid to rest.[26]

THE DEMISE OF CAHOKIA

Sometime after AD 1200, the great metropolis of Cahokia was abandoned, as was its northern outpost, Aztalan. By AD 1400, the Mississippian civilization disappeared from the Midwest and the heart of this remarkable culture had shifted south. This civilization vanished so completely in the Midwest we do not even know what language the Mississippians of Cahokia spoke.

We do not know why Cahokia collapsed but there are many theories. Among these are disease, depletion of resources, degradation of the environment due to vast clearing of land, climatic change that affected crops and other resources, persistent warfare, and internal political instability. Regarding climate change, it has long been noted that the demise of Cahokia and the Mississippians in the Upper Midwest is correlated with the end of a long warm and wet period and the beginning of a cooler climate, right around AD 1200. Climatic studies around Cahokia itself suggest that the warm, moist weather pattern ended with a long drought that could have affected the agricultural economy.[27] Simulations by University of Wisconsin–Madison climatologists also model a temporary drop in precipitation beginning circa AD 1100 in parts of the Upper Midwest that would include Aztalan,[28] but the consequences of the modeled precipitation change have not been studied.

It may be that all of these factors contributed to the demise of Cahokia. People continued to live in the general region after abandonment of the city, and almost certainly among them were the descendants of the early Mississippians themselves. But North America never again saw the splendor of this ancient capital.

THREE

The Cultural Landscape

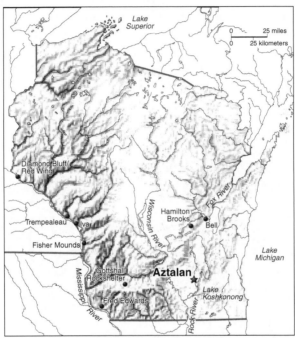

Figure 3.1. Map showing locations of archaeological sites related to
Late Woodland, Oneota, and Mississippian Cultures

WISCONSIN AT AD 1000–1200

The Mississippians who migrated north into what is now Wisconsin to
establish the town of Aztalan did not enter vacant country. Two other
Indian peoples shared the landscape of southern Wisconsin during the life of
the Aztalan community and their histories are interwoven with that of the
Mississippians of Aztalan. The first group consisted of many bands or tribes
of people called Late Woodland by archaeologists. Late Woodland refers to
a period and way of life that lasted from AD 500 to about AD 1200 in some
places. The second group was the Oneota who suddenly appeared (relatively
speaking) in the archaeological record after about AD 1100. The lifestyle
and customs of the Oneota people persisted into the historic period when

the Europeans encountered the descendants of these people, in the form of several tribes, during the seventeenth century.

PEOPLE OF THE LATE WOODLAND

The Late Woodland is an outgrowth of earlier Woodland cultures that appeared two thousand years ago. The earlier part of the Woodland tradition is characterized by people who hunted and gathered for food, buried some of their dead in earthen burial mounds, and produced pottery jars, tempered with crushed rock, and decorated with intricate designs. Late Woodland pottery is distinguished from earlier Woodland periods by elaborate designs impressed with thin cords and woven fabrics. Archaeologists call this characteristic pottery Madison ware (Figure 3.2a).

Figures 3.2a and b. Left: Late Woodland Madison Ware pottery. Right: Late Woodland collared pottery found at Aztalan

The Late Woodland of Wisconsin is best known for the elaboration of an ancient burial mound-building custom. In earlier times, between about 500 BC and AD 500, Woodland people built large conical or round mounds for burial of certain people. Sometime after AD 700, and lasting perhaps to about AD 1150, the Late Woodland people of southern Wisconsin and adjoining states began sculpting hills and other locations into burial mounds and mounds for other purposes in the shapes of natural and supernatural animals important in North American Indian religions. Included are thunderbirds and hawks, bears, and a variety of long-tailed spirit beings that inhabit the watery underworld, referred to as underground water panthers and water spirits. Some linear mounds, the long cigar-shaped mounds that many times accompany more recognizable effigy mounds, may represent snakes, important denizens of the lower world for many Indian cultures, including, as we have seen, the Mississippians. In *Indian Mounds of Wisconsin,* Birmingham and Eisenberg refer to these astonishing effigy mound groups as "cosmological maps" of Late Woodland belief systems.[1] Nearly one thousand different effigy mound groups were built in Wisconsin alone, including more than fifteen thousand small conical, effigy, and linear mounds.

We do not know why these people placed symbols of their beliefs so prominently on the landscape. Perhaps it is no coincidence that much effigy mound construction appears to have occurred between AD 800 and 1100, bracketing the emergence of corn agriculture and the emergence of other new societies elsewhere in the Upper Midwest. Indeed, there is good evidence that some Late Woodland effigy mound builders began growing corn themselves after about AD 900. Quite possibly, effigy mound construction represents the formation of a new ethnic group—a tribe or confederation of tribes—with the effigy mound groups serving as ceremonial centers to reinforce group identity. The formation of this new culture could well have been a social response to the great cultural changes sweeping over the Midwest at this time.

Effigy mound groups, camps, and villages were once common in the Rock River drainage and along the Crawfish River. One of the largest concentrations of effigy mounds in this part of the state was along the shores of nearby Lake Koshkonong where almost two dozen large effigy mound groups could once be found overlooking the lake.[2] Directly across the river from Aztalan are the earthworks noted by Lewis and Barrett that include a large long-tailed effigy mound, one hundred feet long, believed to represent one of the underground water panthers or water spirits. Such creatures are characteristically associated with water bodies, and especially springs—entrances to the watery underworld for this spirit. This long-tailed mound is pointed directly at a major spring complex on the opposite side of the river. It is not yet known if the earthwork was made before Aztalan or if it formed a ceremonial place for local allies just outside of the great walls.

After about AD 1000, archaeologists see significant changes in the economy and customs of Late Woodland populations of southeastern Wisconsin, extending as far north as the Door Peninsula on Green Bay. Corn was now commonly grown. Habitation sites consisted of small, but substantially built houses and underground storage pits for crops and other food. Some sites have houses with a curious "keyhole" shape and, like those found in many other regions at the time, these were semi-subterranean pit houses, dug several feet into the ground, with wooden pole and bark walls and roofing (Figure 3.3). Some of the villages were fortified with log stockades indicating the threat of attack. The rims and necks of the cord-decorated pottery jars are similar to effigy mound ceramics in many ways, but are now greatly thickened at the rim with a collar-like addition.

Two theories account for these changes in the Late Woodland culture. For archaeologist Philip Salkin, president of Archaeological Consulting and Services, the corn-growing Late Woodland people who made collared ceramics were a whole new people who appeared around AD 800 and, at least for a time, lived side by side with the effigy mound builders. He places these new people into an archaeological classification different from the effigy

Figure 3.3. Remains of a Late Woodland key-hole shaped house at the Statz Site

mound people—the Kekoskee Phase of the Late Woodland Stage. He does not believe that the Kekoskee people built effigy mounds because their camps and villages are not usually found near effigy mound groups. While Salkin thinks that the Kekoskee people could have been drawn from local populations, he also thinks it is possible that they represent new people who came into Wisconsin during a wave of migration from the south, a view shared by some others.[3]

Others see the Kekoskee people as none other than the effigy mound builders who, in some areas, were adapting to changes brought about by corn agriculture. Increasing reliance on corn would have allowed for larger, more permanent villages and gradually eliminated the need for social and mortuary gatherings at special ceremonial centers. The addition of collars to the pots may simply have been a practical change—strengthening the necks and rims of the pots for lifting them in and out of underground storage pits that had become common as the need for food storage increased. In contrast, the earlier effigy mound Madison ware pots have very thin rims and necks that probably would have broken easily with constant handling.

The distribution of the new collared ceramics on sites over the Upper Midwest suggests that cultural changes during the Late Woodland in Wisconsin do not necessarily reflect migrations of new people. Several studies of this distribution demonstrate that the *main* concentration of collared pottery types in the Upper Midwest is, in fact, found in southeastern and eastern Wisconsin, not more southerly areas, the previously proposed origin place of this pottery.[4] Collared pots even accompany a few burials in Wisconsin effigy mounds, further suggesting that the effigy mound builders and the Kekoskee people could have been one and the same, but the issue is still not settled.

ONEOTA

Between AD 1100 and 1200, the distinctive customs, including burial mounds and pottery that define all Late Woodland groups, disappear from the archaeological record in southern Wisconsin and are completely replaced with a new lifestyle archaeologists call Oneota. The culture of the Oneota was different from both the Late Woodland people and the Mississippians, although it contained some attributes of both. Many, in fact, think the Oneota was born from the cultural and biological union of Mississippian and local Late Woodland groups beginning about AD 1050–1150. The situation is complex and hotly debated, but many agree that *among* the descendants of the Oneota in Wisconsin are the Chiwere Sioux-speaking nations of the Ioway, Ho-Chunk or Winnebago, Oto, and Missouri.

The Oneota lifestyle differed from the Late Woodland in many respects. The sometimes fortified Oneota villages were very much larger than Late Woodland sites and were occupied much of the year. Early Oneota houses were wigwam style but over the centuries evolved into huge "longhouses" that were more than one hundred feet long. The Oneota were farmers but also relied on game, especially deer, fish, clams, and other wild foods. People living near the banks of the Mississippi River traveled west onto the Great Plains for seasonal bison hunts. Oneota hoes were frequently made from bison shoulder blades, apparently acquired during these hunts.

Like the Mississippians, and unlike the Late Woodland people, the Oneota made pottery tempered with crushed shell and decorated with incised or trailed designs (Figure 3.4). Mississippian influence is evident on a few early Oneota pots in the form of ceramic designs such as interlocking scrolls. Falcon symbolism on pots, stone tablets, and rock art continued through the Oneota period. This may also be a legacy of Mississippian contact and influence.

Figure 3.4. Oneota pottery

However, unlike the Mississippians, the Oneota did not build platform mounds nor appear to have had a hierarchical social structure. Some Oneota apparently made small conical mounds for burials, much like their probable Woodland ancestors. Later, the Oneota mainly buried their dead in below-ground cemeteries, unmarked by earthen constructions, although use of burial mounds may have continued in some areas.

Oneota village sites are not found throughout the southern Wisconsin landscape but rather are concentrated in four specific regions: the Lake Pepin area along the Mississippi River; in and around the present city of La Crosse, also on the Mississippi River; along the upper Fox River and the Green Bay of Lake Michigan in east-central Wisconsin; and on Lake Koshkonong just south of Aztalan. Significantly, these are all areas for which there is evidence for an early Mississippian presence.

There are three main theories about the origins of the Oneota. The earliest explanation, now discounted, suggested that the Oneota were the Mississippians themselves who migrated north and adopted a simpler lifestyle. The second idea developed by long-time Oneota researcher, David Overstreet, a founder of the Great Lakes Archaeological Research Center, is that the Oneota derived from southern horticultural populations who, like some Late Woodland people, moved north into Wisconsin prior to the Mississippians.[5] In this thinking, the Oneota culture expanded, displacing the Late Woodland people, including the effigy mound builders.

A last theory, supported by many and advanced by James Stoltman, professor emeritus at the University of Wisconsin–Madison, is that the Wisconsin Oneota are none other than the recent descendants of local Late Woodland people—the effigy mound builders and the succeeding Kekoskee people.[6] Stoltman argues that the adoption of corn agriculture and contact with Mississippian customs and technology stimulated the evolution of one lifestyle into the other. In Stoltman's view, contact with the Mississippians occurred both indirectly through trade and ceremonial interactions, and directly through the presence of the Mississippians themselves, notably at Aztalan. He also thinks that many Late Woodland people of the area physically moved to Mississippian trade and ceremonial centers located at various strategic places, abandoning former lifestyles in the process.

THE MISSISSIPPIANS IN WISCONSIN

We do not know why the Mississippians moved north into Wisconsin but it is a matter of great research interest. Again, there are several hypotheses. One is that Cahokia attempted to gain political and ideological control of the northern frontier. However, most experts doubt that the city had enough centralized political power to mount such an invasion. Another possibility is the Mississippians, such as those at Aztalan, were breakaway groups from the populous Cahokia region who moved north to establish their own chiefdoms and communities. Indeed, archaeologists detect a substantial reduction in the population of the Cahokia area a little after the time the Mississippians came to Aztalan.[7]

Another explanation is that Mississippians expanded trade networks into the north to get necessities and symbolic items not immediately available to either those at Cahokia or others in the Cahokian sphere of influence. Initial interest in the northern frontier apparently focused on such items as lead for white paint, found in the southwestern part of the state; a rock from west-central Wisconsin called Hixton Silicified Sandstone that had great symbolic importance; deer meat and hides from the vast and productive deer country, and other food from the same area; and perhaps even wild rice.[8] Getting copper from northern Michigan quarries almost certainly would have involved Wisconsin people as well.

Whatever the case, some northern archaeological sites show unmistakable evidence of communication with the American Bottom after about AD 1000 and this evidence increases over the next century as Cahokia itself came into power. An even earlier link between the people of the south and the indigenous Late Woodland effigy mound people may be found at Gottschall Rockshelter, in the uplands above the Wisconsin River in southwestern Wisconsin. Located near one of the largest and most unusual effigy mound group concentrations, now called the Eagle Township mound complex, the cave walls bear spectacular paintings rendered in an unmistakable artistic style associated with later Mississippians (Figure 3.5).[9] Oddly, no southern

Figure 3.5. The Gottschall Rockshelter paintings are rendered in Mississippian artistic style and may represent stories associated with the culture hero Red Horn.

Illinois or Mississippian artifacts have been found in the cave. Instead, site excavator, Robert Salzer, head of Cultural Landscape Legacies, links the paintings to a layer of deposits with Late Woodland effigy mound pottery dating prior to AD 1000.

Robert Hall, along with Salzer, believes the paintings depict a story associated with the ancient Native American culture hero Red Horn.[10] The paintings feature Mississippian warriors including one, possibly one of Red Horn's sons, adorned as a falcon-warrior with long-nosed god maskettes tattooed or painted on his chest. They believe that Gottschall was a ritual cave used for ceremonies to form alliances between Late Woodland and Mississippian peoples through elaborate kinship adoption ceremonies.

Many other Wisconsin sites trace the increasing influence Cahokia had on its northern frontier between AD 1100 and 1200, as well as movements of the Mississippians themselves north into the region. Almost every year new sites are found. Much of the evidence is in the form of Mississippian pottery and other artifacts such as distinctive arrowheads and ornaments. About AD 1100, the beautifully made and ceremonially important Mississippian pottery, Ramey Incised, appeared in places.

Among the earlier Mississippian sites in Wisconsin is the only other platform mound complex known in Wisconsin aside from Aztalan. This complex was built on a high hill overlooking the Mississippi River and the present town of Trempealeau (Figure 3.6). Archaeologists have not yet found a

Figure 3.6. Early 20th century photo of Trempealeau platform mounds on a high hill near the Mississippi River

village associated with these platform mounds but they have found early Mississippian pottery sherds in the area.[11] Additionally, about twelve miles to the south, near the city of La Crosse, archaeologists of the Mississippi Valley Archaeology Center found later Mississippian pottery intermixed with Late Woodland pottery along with other Mississippian artifacts. At the Iva site, discovered in 2003, researchers from the Mississippi Valley Archaeology Center found Ramey Incised pottery as well as other Mississippian pottery types and earspools—the hallmark of Mississippian warriors and elite. In the same part of the state, near Stoddard, Wisconsin, archaeological excavations at the Fisher Mounds site found pottery and stone artifacts made of rock that originated in southern Illinois.[12]

Other sites track physical movements of Mississippians into Wisconsin. The Fred Edwards site on the Grant River in southwestern Wisconsin, for example, was a temporary village, fortified by a wooden pole stockade that dates to between AD 1050 and 1150. Pottery from the site includes a large representation of Mississippian styles, including Ramey Incised, as well as Late Woodland types thought to have originated among people from Iowa and northern Illinois. Lead, deer bone, and hide scrapers in comparatively high numbers led University of Wisconsin–Madison archaeologists Fred Finney and James Stoltman to conclude that Mississippians and their trading allies came here to acquire deer hides and lead, either for Cahokia itself or for other people in the Mississippian trade network.[13]

Farther north along the Mississippi River, near what is today Red Wing, Minnesota, and Diamond Bluff, Wisconsin, archaeologists defined a huge site complex of villages that show interesting mixtures of artifacts and features. The villages include platform mounds on the Minnesota side, and thousands of small burial mounds, including a few effigy mounds, Oneota pottery, and Mississippian artifacts such as pottery and a long-nosed god maskette. Mississippians seem to have moved to this area, and the villages seem to have been populated by former Woodland people in the process of becoming "Mississippianized" into what is now called Oneota. The admixture of Indian cultures in the process of cultural change is captured in a remarkable feature in one of the area villages: a classic long-tailed Late Woodland effigy mound with grave offerings of Oneota and Mississippian-like pottery.[14]

The Mississippians were especially active in eastern Wisconsin between AD 1050 and 1200, but here also the evidence includes villages of mixed populations. One important village, as yet not thoroughly investigated, is the Hamilton-Brooks site located eighty miles north of Aztalan on the Fox River, near the modern town of Berlin. Archaeologists sampling the site found both Woodland and Mississippian pottery in an apparently fortified village. This Fox River location seems strategic. The river flows diagonally across the state, from its headwaters near the Wisconsin River to the Green Bay of Lake Michigan. A short and famous portage links the Fox to the Wisconsin River and the Mississippi River drainage system. Because of this connection, the Fox River was always a vital transportation and trade route and much fought over.

Five hundred years later, the Fox or Mesquakie nation, from which the river takes its name, maintained fortified villages along the river to control the French fur trade traffic, leading to a devastating war with the French. One such stockaded village, now called the Bell site, is thought to have been the grand village of the Fox, attacked by the French in the early 1700s. It is located upstream from Hamilton-Brooks on Lake Butte des Morts, a large widening in the Fox River. Here, University of Wisconsin–Oshkosh archaeologist Jeffery Behm made a surprise discovery—a much earlier occupation at the site included Mississippian pottery and the people of this earlier occupation could have been responsible for some of the fortifications found at the site.[15] Perhaps, like the later Fox, the Mississippians and their allies sought to control this important waterway.

On Lake Koshkonong, another strategic location along the Rock River, Oneota villages replaced effigy mound camps and mound groups. The earliest of these new villages seem to have had close relationships with the emerging Mississippian civilization as indicated by Mississippian-like pottery designs and other cultural traits such as Cahokia-like house forms.[16] Sometime between AD 1050 and 1100, a group of Mississippian people moved to a nearby village of Late Woodland allies on the Crawfish River, a tributary of the Rock River, and built the first and only Mississippian ceremonial town in Wisconsin, heavily fortified by huge walls of timber and clay.

FOUR

Aztalan: A Mississippian Town

────◆•◄►•◆────

With this cultural and historical background, we now move to the banks of the Crawfish River to examine the site of Aztalan itself, its environment, history, and how it appeared nine hundred years ago.

ENVIRONMENT

Aztalan is located on the west bank of the Crawfish River, a tributary of the Rock River that in turn flows southwesterly into the Mississippi River at Rock Island, Illinois (Figure 4.1). Theoretically, one could launch a canoe at

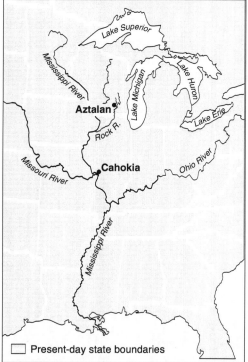

Figure 4.1. Map showing location of Aztalan in relation to Cahokia

the site and travel entirely by water to Cahokia itself. Whether or not the Mississippians did this routinely is open to question because some think that enemy villages on Lake Koshkonong, a widening of the Rock River about fifteen miles from Aztalan, would have prevented safe passage along that part of the route.

During the life of the town, this part of Wisconsin offered ample and highly diverse resources for Indian people. The mosaic of woodlands, prairie, and parklands in southern Wisconsin, for example, provided some of the best habitat for deer in the Upper Midwest. The deer herd appears to have been enormous. In most ancient camps and villages that archaeologists have examined in the region, deer is by far the largest category of food.

Streams, lakes, and vast wetlands, characteristic of southeastern Wisconsin, provided large quantities of fish and clams. The lakes and wetlands also supported dense stands of wild rice that attracted huge flocks of waterfowl because the region is part of the great Mississippi flyway. When the first Euro-American explorers came to nearby Lake Koshkonong, they described it as a wild rice "meadow." Aztalan is ideally situated for access to such resources—it is located above a large widening of the river that may have been a large shallow lake at the time. Other wild foods found in the immediate area of the site include several varieties of high protein nuts, and over forty-five edible plants.[1]

Timber for building and firewood would have been abundant on the east side of the river where there were once forests of oak, maple, beech, and basswood. Elsewhere in the immediate vicinity grew prairie grass, cattail rushes, and sedge that supplied thatch and material for matting. For Indian farmers, the soils of the Crawfish River floodplain were fertile, well drained, and tillable using available technology.

Aside from the rich resource base of the region, several other environmental and cultural factors would have made Aztalan a strategic and otherwise ideal location for a town. Prairie and small stands of trees, called oak openings, dominated the west side of the river where the town was built, eliminating the need for extensive clearing. This stretch of the Crawfish River is both narrow and shallow, providing a ford for crossing. Old Indian trails crossed the river at this location and the nineteenth-century pioneer town of Aztalan developed here because of the ford. A main bridge across the river is still located at the north end of ancient Aztalan.

The narrow and shallow stream configuration made the location ideal for the construction of fish dams or weirs for the seasonal capture of huge quantities of fish. The Indians built a wall of stone, usually V-shaped, just below the surface of the water with a small opening at the center. Spawning fish crowded into the opening, seeking their way upstream, and could have been easily speared in vast numbers. Native Americans widely used fish dams in ancient and modern times right into the twentieth century. In addition to the dam at Aztalan, another dam was photographed by Aztalan park naturalist, Tom Davies, just north of the site during a drought that lowered the river in 2003 (Figures 4.2a and c). There is a third Crawfish River fish dam located a few miles upstream at the present day town of Milford.

Figures 4.2a and b. Remnants of a fish dam at Aztalan on the Crawfish River and a drawing of a Native American spear fishing

Large springs flow along this stretch of the Crawfish River that would have not only provided fresh water but made the river in this section less susceptible to freezing. Spring waters are important to Native American religious practices in which they represent life, rebirth, and renewal, and are viewed as entrances to the watery underworld for powerful medicine animals. Effigy mound groups are many times located at prominent and presumably sacred springs.[2] The ancient town of Aztalan enclosed springs within its walls and these provided access to water even if the town was under attack.

Figure 4.2c. Virtually intact fish dam upstream on the Crawfish River (upper right)

HISTORY

The ancient town was not the first Indian community here. People lived here, at least for short periods of time, over ten thousand years. Intermixed with the town debris, archaeologists have found stone tools, pottery, and other distinctive artifacts from many previous cultures.[3]

Some of the evidence indicates that people gathered here for more than just subsistence activities. For example, Barrett illustrates a platform pipe in *Ancient Aztalan* that is now linked to Middle Woodland people who used the area 800–1000 years before the Mississippian town.[4] Such pipes are connected to a ceremonial tradition called Hopewell found throughout the Midwest: the pipes themselves were frequently included in the burial mounds of high status people at ceremonial centers. Some of the mounds and other earthworks surrounding Aztalan may date to this period. Others could have been destroyed as the ancient town expanded.

The giant long-tailed effigy mound near the small enclosures on the east bank of the Crawfish may predate the Mississippians and indicates that the place continued to be a ceremonial place important to the indigenous Late Woodland people. Elsewhere in Wisconsin, effigy mound construction ceased by AD 1100 or not long after the appearance of the Mississippians.

The most valuable insight into the history of the town itself comes from excavations in a refuse accumulation or midden along the river just inside the main walls, first identified by Barrett and excavated in the 1980s by the University of Wisconsin–Milwaukee. Here, archaeologist John Richards found layers of garbage that began to accumulate between AD 800 and 900 and continued throughout the life of the town.[5] The deposits are an Aztalan history book, encapsulated and preserved by a thick layer of eroded topsoil from modern farming.

Richards concluded that the community began as a Late Woodland farming village, perhaps extending all along the Crawfish River at this point. The inhabitants made Late Woodland kinds of collared and cord-impressed pottery. Like some other researchers, Richards thinks that some of these Late Woodland people migrated north into Wisconsin from northern Illinois as part of an initial expansion of Woodland people following the adoption of corn agriculture.

Whether or not this was the case, the people that settled at Aztalan had connections to the emerging Mississippian civilization to the south. In the soil layer dating to just before AD 1100, pottery similar to early Mississippian styles was found mixed with the Late Woodland pottery. Some of the pottery seems to be locally made copies rather than trade vessels. Richards named one of these pottery types, Hyer Plain, after the man who first brought Aztalan to the public's attention.

Sometime close to about AD 1100, Mississippians themselves arrived. Distinctive Mississippian pottery appears in the layers of town debris that date to this time period. At the same time, a thick layer of topsoil that washed down from the site above suggests extensive clearing and building activities that led to soil erosion. A section of the new town wall was built over the old dump. The archaeologists also found Late Woodland pottery in these layers, supporting evidence found elsewhere on the site that Aztalan was an ethnically diverse community.

Richards thinks that the Mississippian people came directly from Cahokia itself based on close similarities in the pottery and other artifacts and features at the site. This is supported by James Stoltman's analysis of the clay from some of the pots that traces the pots' origins to the Cahokia area.[6] Other experts, like Lynne Goldstein and Robert Hall, point to areas farther north in the Mississippian sphere of influence as the possible homeland.

We may never know what specifically brought the Mississippians to the banks of the Crawfish at this time and to this particular Late Woodland village. Obviously these were allies. The population of Cahokia itself seems to drop dramatically at or by AD 1100 and possibly Aztalan reflects this dispersal. Some Cahokia experts point to general population expansion and/or internal factional disputes as likely reasons for northern settlement at Aztalan. Or, given the unstable and violent nature of the times, trade networks consisting of non-Mississippian middlemen may have become unstable. If the Mississippians came to regain control of trading routes established earlier, moving in with allies and building a large formidable presence would seem logical. Although nearby Lake Koshkonong would seem a more likely location for a town, a new group living there, the Oneota, may not have been welcoming.

Study of the riverside deposits at Aztalan supports earlier interpretations that sometime around AD 1200 the town was abandoned and no one occupied the area for many centuries afterward. This is about the same time that Cahokia archaeologists note that the city was clearly in demise but not yet totally abandoned. According to present evidence, the Mississippians themselves may have lived at Aztalan for only a century or so.

A PLANNED COMMUNITY

Like other Mississippian towns, the layout of Aztalan mirrored the social structure and belief systems of its people. The overall plan of Aztalan was rectangular, lying parallel to the Crawfish River, and surrounded by huge wood and clay walls with an oblong enclosure at its southwest corner. Like Cahokia, platform mounds were oriented to the cardinal directions. As elsewhere in the Mississippian world, the town was divided into three major zones or precincts—residential, public plaza, and elite—as well as other activity areas.

The residential areas in many later Mississippian towns encircled the central plazas, reserved for public ceremonies, and the plazas were bordered by platform mounds and elite buildings and houses (Figure 4.3). At Aztalan, the Mississippians used the local topography to arrange space. The residential area or precinct was low along the river and the elite precinct was on the high ridge above. The Mississippians placed the plaza between these two areas. This water-to-sky arrangement, with intermediating ceremonial grounds and people, modeled the layered Mississippian universe. Massive walls separated the three zones, with the plaza and elite precincts forming semi-concentric rings around the general population so that the people in these areas also had access to the river. The interior walls partitioned the site into social spaces, but several lines of interior walls also would have been useful as backup defensive measures, should the main wall be breached during attack.

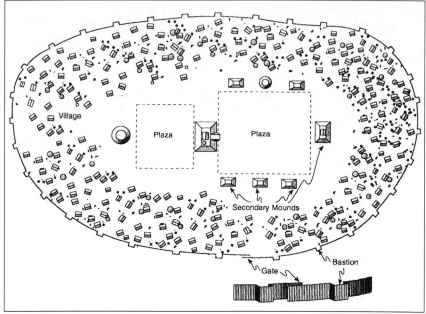

Figure 4.3. Plan of typical late Mississippian community from Lewis, Stout, and Wesson (1998)

The nature and arrangement of access points reflect tight social control and a defensive posture. A small number of narrow passageways or gateways regulated traffic between the precincts. Such control of social space was characteristic of Mississippian towns into the historic period. The types of gateways found at Aztalan include narrow gaps in the wall, overlapping walls, and "wing gates" that funneled people, practically single file, into log post passageways (Figure 4.4). Many gateways were located adjacent to the bastions where presumably they would have been well guarded. Both the elite and the people from the residential precincts had access to the plaza, but the people living along the river apparently could not directly approach the western platform mounds. Small entrances to Aztalan have been identified for the eastern, riverside wall, and the elite precinct and seem to have had separate and restricted access ways to the river and the outside world at the northeast corner of the town. One additional wing gate in the north wall in this area linked the elite precinct to the agricultural fields immediately north of the town.

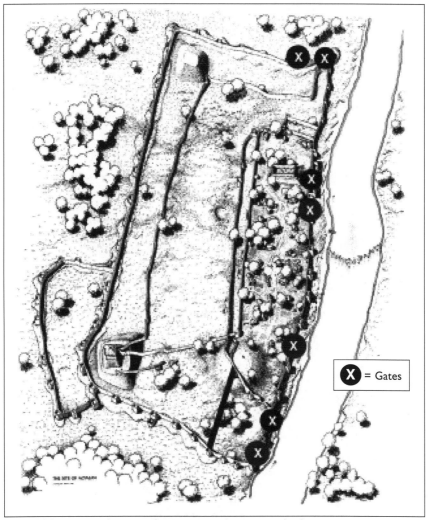

Figure 4.4. Approximate locations of various external gateways at Aztalan

Excavations into the platform mounds reveal that Aztalan underwent at least three expansions or building episodes. In the Mississippian world, periodic expansions and rebuilding accompanied world renewal ceremonies often associated with the death of a chief.[7] Among the Natchez, for example, the chiefly residence was burned at the death of the chief, and a new mound was built over the spot for the house of the new leader. If this was the case at Aztalan, the town underwent at least three changes in leadership, a reasonable succession number if the Mississippians lived here for about a century.

A TOUR OF THE TOWN

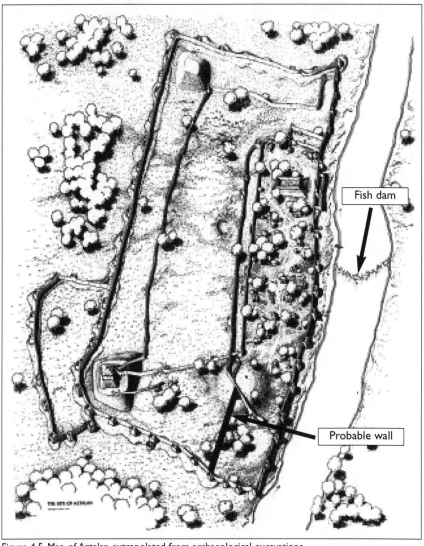

Figure 4.5. Map of Aztalan extrapolated from archaeological excavations

The Walls

> . . . *the walls are made in this fashion. They drive stakes tall and straight close together. These are then interlaced with long withes, and then overlain by clay within and without. They make loopholes at intervals and make their towers and turrets separated by a curtain and parts of a wall as seems best. And at a distance it seems like a fine wall or rampart and such stockades are very strong.*[8]

In the sixteenth century, a member of the infamous De Soto expedition provided this description of a wall around an abandoned Indian town along the Alabama River. It also serves as a good description of the great exterior walls of Aztalan, where we begin a tour of the site (Figure 4.5). Enclosing twenty-one acres, the tall Aztalan walls were supported by thirty-two evenly spaced rectangular bastions or watchtowers. These structures not only functioned as defensive positions but also buttressed the massive wood and clay walls. The thick layer of clay mixed with grass, which coated the walls, would have given the town walls an impressive adobe-like appearance (Figure 4.6). In practical terms, the clay coating would have preserved the timber from rot and served as a fire retardant.

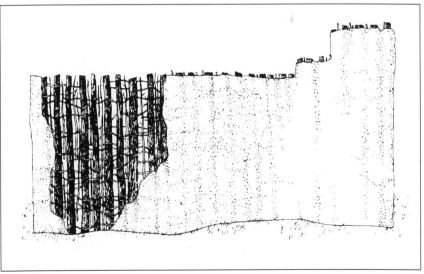

Figure 4.6. Wisconsin Historical Society drawing of wall construction

The Residential Precinct

The heart of the town was the residential zone or precinct located next to the Crawfish River (Figure 4.7). Most of the population lived here, completely enclosed by massive timber and clay walls. The western side of the enclosure consisted of double walls, either the result of expansions or built as an extra defensive measure to protect the bulk of the Aztalan population.

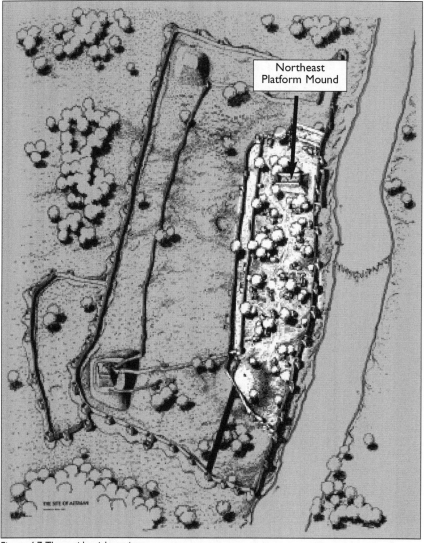

Figure 4.7. The residential precinct

At the north end of this precinct, the people maintained a council house and temple. At the south end, on and around a large oval natural knoll, early archaeologists discovered an unusual mortuary or human bone disposal area. The walls of the residential precinct enclosed at least one large spring that had been paved with stone, evidently to secure footing.

To date, archaeologists have identified at least fifteen houses in the residential precinct. These were small circular and rectangular pit houses framed by upright poles and roofed with thatch or bark (Figures 4.8, 4.9). The walls of the Aztalan houses were constructed using the wattle and daub technique, similar to the construction of the walls around the town; the clay coatings helped to waterproof and insulate the structures. Protected entranceways kept wind, rain, and snow from house interiors, and house entrances faced south, away from cold north winds.

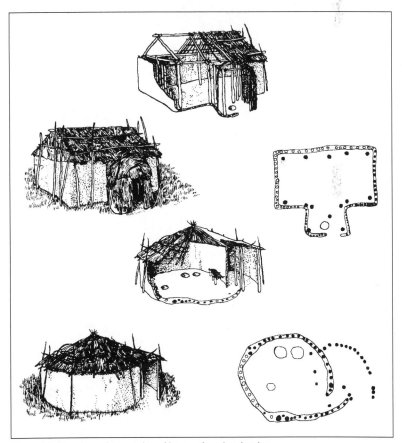

Figure 4.8. Drawings of two styles of houses found at Aztalan

Figure 4.9. Kenosha Public Museum mural of scene from residential district looking northwest to mortuary mound

Houses at Aztalan were small, single-family structures enclosing only about four hundred square feet.[9] Characteristically, the houses contained only a fire pit and a few small storage pits. They were probably only used for sleeping and as shelters from foul weather. Much of the daily activities, including food preparation, took place outside. Extrapolating from the density of known houses to the rest of the residential area, Richards estimates a population of about 300–350 people.[10] Throughout the residential zone, archaeologists discovered fireplaces, roasting pits, storage and refuse pits, shell heaps, small dumps of stone tool chipping debris, and post patterns that represent other activities. Several large concentrations of burned and cracked rocks may be the remnants of sweat lodges, common features in Native American villages and towns. Barrett also documented one odd U-shaped pattern of rocks. One pit feature contained a large concentration of clam shells probably being stored for use in pottery manufacture. The Mississippians tempered their fine pots with crushed clam shell.

One closely spaced pattern of post molds, discovered by Barrett, outlined an interesting circular structure, twenty feet in diameter, without a detectable entrance (Figure 4.10). The structure would have been too small and the posts too closely spaced to have been used as a "woodhenge," and Barrett noted that it lacked a fire pit and other signs of use as a habitation. This may have been a ceremonial structure or even a large version of a circular raised corn granary like those occasionally found at Cahokia-era sites and described for later Mississippian towns.[11] Raised several feet off the ground to prevent rodent intrusions, these silo-like structures stored corn for communal consumption. One clue that may help solve the mystery of this structure is its location. It was placed between a network of passageways in the north wall of the residential area leading to the plaza and the town's main ceremonial structure, the temple.

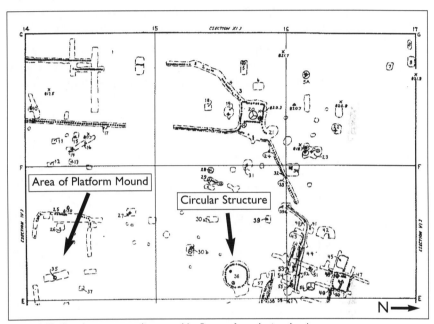

Figure 4.10. Circular structure discovered by Barrett from *Ancient Aztalan*

THE NORTHEAST PLATFORM MOUND

This temple, the front of which looks towards the rising sun, is placed on a mound of dirt brought hither that rises about 8 feet above the natural level of the ground on the bank of a little river. The mound loses itself in an insensible slope on the side towards the square . . . The eternal fire is kept in this first part of the temple.[12]

—Le Page du Pratz at an eighteenth-century Natchez town

Near the northeast corner of the residential area, the Aztalan Indians built a large structure on a low rectangular platform mound that no doubt functioned as a council house or temple typically found in Mississippian communities.[13] The platform mound was nearly identical to the Natchez temple mound described above, built hundreds of years later. The sacred fires of the towns were kept burning in these structures, and sometimes the structures contained the bones of chiefs as well as sacred objects. Special guardians kept the fires. Among some groups, the guardians could not let the fire go out under penalty of death.

Unfortunately, plowing damaged the northeast mound at Aztalan and twentieth-century archaeological field parties could barely make out the northeast mound that was clearly shown on Lapham's 1855 map. Lapham's map indicates that it was wedge-shaped and oriented in an east-west direction (Figure 4.11). It stood about five feet high at its east end and, exactly like the temple described by the French observer, the Aztalan temple mound

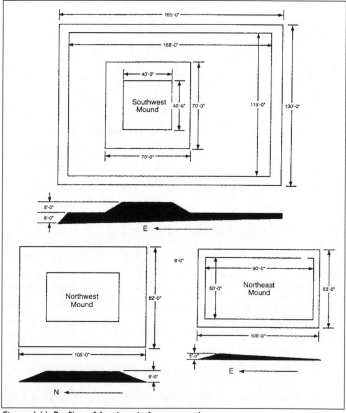

Figure 4.11. Profiles of Aztalan platform mounds

sloped in the direction of the plaza. Curiously, at least at one point in the town's history, a double wall seems to have stood between this mound and the plaza.

Archaeologists located the remains of the temple and determined that it underwent one rebuilding on the same spot.[14] It began its existence as a large open-walled, vertical post structure, forty-five by ninety feet in size, built on the ground surface cleared of sod. It was probably roofed with thatch, and mats covered the spaces between the vertical posts of the walls. Sometime later, the town's people dismantled the building and built the low platform mound and a structure upon it, identical in size to the original structure. The structures enclosed pits that archaeologists found filled with charcoal interspersed with white sand, a purifying material in the belief systems of Native Americans. These pits were probably the locations of Aztalan's sacred town fire. (Figure 4.12)

Figure 4.12. Maintenance of the sacred fire on the temple mound

Mortuary Areas

Near the center of the residential precinct, Barrett found one feature that appears to have been a crematory. This was a clay "bathtub-shaped" receptacle containing a narrow firebox with partly burned human remains mixed with charcoal and ash (Figure 4.13). Alongside this feature, Barrett found over eighty arrowheads in a large area of charcoal; this was possibly an offering.

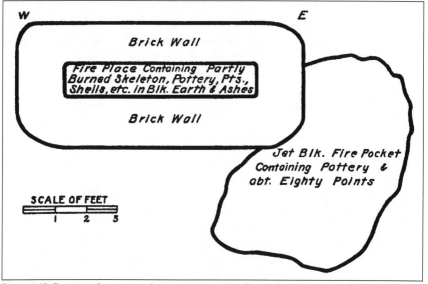

Figure 4.13. Drawing of crematory feature discovered by Barrett from *Ancient Aztalan*

At the southern end of the residential precinct there is a natural glacial knoll. Walls separating this precinct from other areas of the town crossed a portion of the knoll. East of this knoll, near the river, Barrett uncovered numerous trash pits and fire pits that contained dismembered human remains—skulls, limbs, and other body parts that were cut, broken, cracked, charred, and mixed in with other refuse. This, and other such evidence at the site, prompted Barrett to mistakenly call the town's people cannibals. Most of the knoll itself has not been examined, but testing by Barrett also uncovered several formal burial pits. This knoll may in fact be the "large oval mound" from which Sterling reported finding many tied bone bundles in 1838. Supported by modern forensic analysis, Goldstein, who also has studied Mississippian mortuary patterns, has concluded that much of this was a by-product of the extensive processing of bone that the Mississippian people practiced as part of protracted mortuary rituals. However, the treatment of some of the remains also suggests that some of the people represented could have been victims of violence.

The Plaza

> *On the plain at the foot of a hill, natural or artificial, they make a square plaza . . . surrounding which the nobles and chief men build their houses*[15]

—Garcilaso de Vega with the De Soto Expedition

Moving west from the enclosed residential precinct nine hundred years ago we would have passed through narrow and guarded gateways in the double wall and entered the second walled precinct—the public plaza (Figure 4.14).

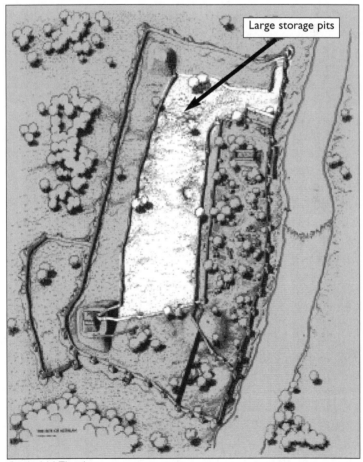

Figure 4.14. The plaza

It is here that people of Aztalan held public ceremonies and feasts and perhaps even played the important chunkey game. The Mississippian Indians of the southeastern United States are known to have continuously maintained plazas, carefully sweeping and leveling the dirt, especially during a cleansing ritual preceding the annual Green Corn ceremony. In some areas of the Aztalan plaza, limited excavations revealed linear and semicircular post patterns, suggesting that at some point, there were houses in this area. These may have been part of a Late Woodland village that existed here before the Mississippian town and construction of the plaza.

At Aztalan, the plaza is L-shaped and covers the center of the site, extending from the southwest platform mound to the northern edge of the plaza where a long narrow extension curves eastward towards the river. These ceremonial grounds were defined by the double western walls of the residential area and the eastern wall of the narrow elite precinct. This eastern wall was found to be of simple single-post construction without a clay coating or supporting bastions. At the southwest corner of the plaza, the western and southern walls extended up and onto the great southwest mound itself to the entrance of an important enclosure or house that once stood on top of an early stage of this mound. These walls formed a ceremonial entranceway to the plaza.

Early on, archaeologists surmised that this mostly level area functioned as a plaza because it lacked visible features seen in other parts of the town. Although archaeological work here has been limited, what has been found is consistent with this interpretation. At the northern end, researchers from the University of Wisconsin–Milwaukee and Michigan State University located a district of large clay-lined storage pits corresponding to an area of pits or depressions noted by Lapham on his 1855 map.[16] These appear to have been communal storage pits used for public feasts that were later filled in with garbage, and in some cases, human remains.

During an unusually dry period in the late 1980s, the surfaces of these pits appeared as discolored ovals in the park grass. Examining an aerial photograph that the archaeologists had arranged to be taken of the site, seventy of these features could be discerned. UW–M and MSU archaeologists excavated fourteen of these pits and discovered that they were typically about eight feet in diameter and eight feet deep, far larger than the household storage pits of the residential precinct (Figure 4.15). The Aztalan people dug these communal storage pits in an area that they had cleared and leveled. They first removed approximately three feet of soil and then sculpted the surface into three tiers. The removed soil could have been used to build the nearby northwest platform mound. Some of the pits may have served several functions, and some were used in mortuary rituals. It is possible that each one of the terraces had a different function. Goldstein has called the complex the "sculptuary."

Figure 4.15. One of the large storage pits at north end of plaza excavated by archaeologists in the 1990s

The Elite Precinct

Moving westward from the plaza, we come to the highest part of the town within the main walls (Figure 4.16). The area between the public plaza and the outer walls seems to have been reserved for the Mississippian chief's family or clan, and perhaps for sacred rituals not shared with the rest of the community. This zone is roughly U-shaped, enclosing the plaza and residential area. A relatively narrow passageway, bordered by the north plaza wall and

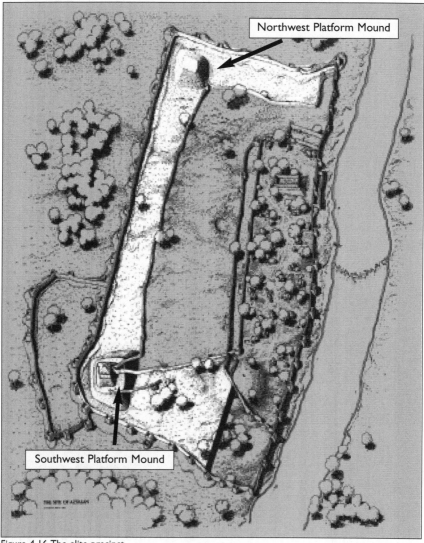

Figure 4.16. The elite precinct

the north exterior wall, runs east to the river and the east exterior wall. The southeast extension of the precinct may have been interrupted by another wall, defining yet another activity area along the river, but this wall has not been completely traced out by archaeologists. As well, archaeologists have not examined the small area created by this suspected barrier so its function is unknown. The only gateway found so far leads to the residential zone. Future work may one day solve the mystery of this southeast area.

At the south end of the narrow elite precinct was the mound associated with the residence of the chiefly family and at the north end, there was a platform mound supporting the mortuary or charnel house for the chieftains and their relatives. Walls running on top of the chiefly mound and a gateway at the base of the mound provided chiefly access to the public ceremonial ground. Additionally, archaeologists have located two other gateways to the plaza, including an odd Z-shaped entranceway (Figure 4.17). Outside access to the elite zone was at the northeast corner of the town, where narrow wing gates led to the river and agricultural fields just north of the town.

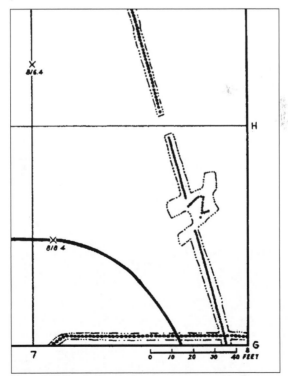

Figure 4.17. Detail of unusual passage way mapped by Barrett between two areas within the site

Except for the walls and the two platform mounds, the elite precinct has not been explored. Drawing upon historical accounts, we would expect houses of other "nobles" to be located here. Lapham mapped a conical mound just north of the southwest platform mound, but the mound disappeared under the plow during the nineteenth century.

THE SOUTHWEST MOUND

. . . it is the custom of the caciques (chiefs) to have their houses on a high hill, made by hand . . .

—De Biedma of the De Soto Expedition in Arkansas[17]

Historical descriptions of Mississippian communities and comparisons to other archaeological sites indicate that principal mounds like the southwest mound of Aztalan, the largest and highest platform mound at the site, supported the residences of the chieftains or lords of Mississippian society. In its final form, the southwest mound was sixteen feet high and consisted of two tiers—a large rectangular basal platform and a square flat-topped pyramid on top (Figure 4.18). The base platform measured 185 by 130 feet. The upper square mound was seventy feet on a side at the base, and about forty feet on a side on the top. A thick layer of light-colored clay coated the top part of the mound, a common feature of chiefly mounds among the Mississippians of the southeastern United States. Appropriately for the "brothers of the sun," the long orientation of the southwest mound faces east, the direction of the rising sun.

Figure 4.18. The reconstructed southwest mound

The mound has not been completed excavated, but extensive digging by Barrett and the Wisconsin Archaeological Survey in 1951 discovered that the mound was built in several phases. The initial platform supported a large ceremonial post in its center that had been burned, consistent with the recorded Mississippian practice of ceremonial burning of structures before rebuilding. Other posts indicate that the people of Aztalan constructed structures on top of at least three later construction stages. On one stage, Barrett described and mapped a square structure, forty-two feet on a side, consisting of walls of large, closely spaced posts that joined the walls of the plaza. There was an entranceway on the east side. The walls of the plaza extended up and onto the top of the southwest platform mound to the entrance of Barrett's log post enclosure. Archaeological evidence suggests these walls were rebuilt several times, expanding or narrowing the entrance to the plaza. It must have been a great spectacle indeed as the great chief emerged from this enclosure to initiate the ceremonies in the plaza, dressed in the colorful trappings of office and framed by the great walls.

Records are unclear as to the shape and nature of the structures on the other stages, although storage pits seemed to have accompanied them. Also unclear is what was inside Barrett's enclosure that rimmed the summit of the mound at one stage in its history. Robert Maher, who led excavations of the mound in 1951, reported finding post molds inside of the enclosure that Barrett excavated but these posts formed no pattern he could discern.[18] Maher speculated that these could be support posts for a house, but could not determine if they were directly associated with the enclosure or later building episodes. At present, we can only say that the structure Barrett found may represent a chiefly house itself, may have enclosed a house, or may have been a sacred enclosure for special activities associated with the elite of Aztalan. Years of plowing greatly damaged any evidence for the appearance of the southwest mound's final stage. Maher found only a layer of ash, the probable remains of a fireplace, on the top of the mound.

MOUND OF THE DEAD: THE NORTHWEST PLATFORM MOUND

Like the southwest mound, the northwest mortuary mound of the elite precinct underwent construction in phases and it consisted of at least two tiers in its finished form. It was at least nine feet high and measured 105 by 92 feet at the base (Figure 4.19). Like the other platform mounds at the site, it is oriented to the cardinal directions. In this case, the long axis is oriented north-south. Although the mound was not entirely excavated, archaeologists identified three construction stages with a small, burned charnel house located on the west side of the second stage (Figure 4.20a, b, and c).[19] Oriented south-

Figure 4.19. The reconstructed northwest mound

east/northwest to the solstices, this structure measured twelve by five feet. It apparently had a small entrance on its southeast side.

Historical accounts describe charnel houses as mausoleums for Mississippian chiefs and members of the chiefly lineage. Periodically, the houses would be burned or emptied of bones that would be reburied elsewhere. The small second stage charnel house at Aztalan, made by wattle and daub construction like Aztalan houses, contained the charred, articulated skeletons of ten men and women, and one other person represented by a bundle of long bones tied with cords. All of these people had been placed, side by side, on a woven cattail mat that formed the floor of the house. Offerings included a ceramic pot and a fabric bag containing hickory nuts. It is possible that the two other construction stages supported similar charnel houses. Lapham reported that human bones and fabric had been found on

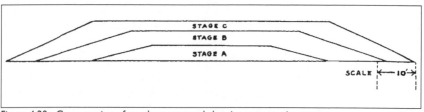

Figure 4.20a. Cross section of northwest mound showing construction stages

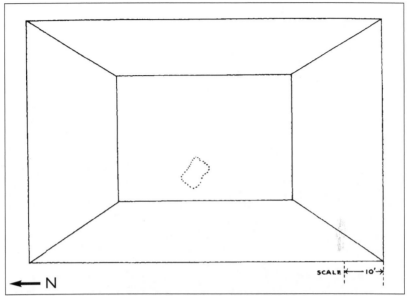

← N

SCALE |←— 10′ —→|

Figure 4.20b. Drawing of the Northwest mound showing location of charnel house. The structure seems oriented southeast to the winter solstice sunrise and northwest to the summer solstice sunset.

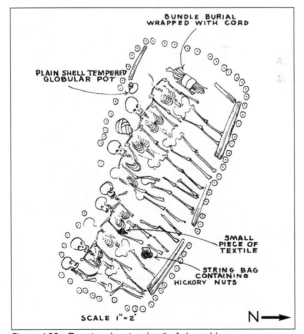

Figure 4.20c. Drawing showing detail of charnel house

the top of this northwest mound; the mound was subsequently disturbed by modern plowing and looting.[20]

The Southwest Enclosure

Walking west from the chiefly mound nine hundred years ago, we would pass through a narrow wing gate in the main wall to the highest point of the town, a ridge that was once surrounded by a mysterious five-acre enclosure extending off the southwest part of the town and the elite precinct (Figure

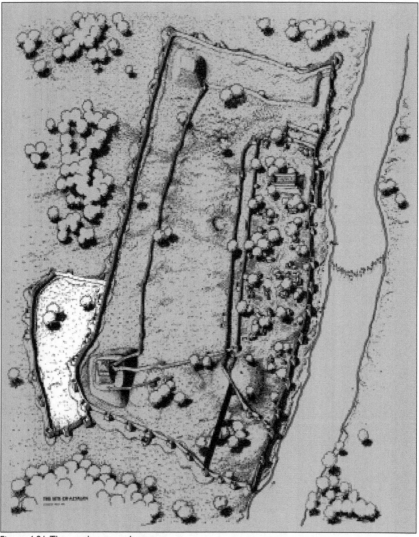

Figure 4.21. The southwest enclosure

4.21). Barrett, and later the Wisconsin Historical Society, excavated all but a small segment of the external enclosure walls and determined that they were built like the main town wall, complete with bastions. They found no exterior exit in the walls that they excavated. However, several narrow gates, including a long wing gate, apparently rebuilt at least once, connected this enclosure to the large southwest platform mound.

The function of this enclosure is a mystery since most of the interior has not been examined. In 1855, Lapham mapped several large earthen features within the boundaries of the enclosure, but these are no longer visible. These included a conical mound, a rise that looked like a conical mound with a long tail, and what appears to have been a segment of yet another bastioned wall running the length of the enclosure. (Figure 4.22) If it was a wall, its location seems to indicate that the enclosure had been rebuilt and expanded

Figure 4.22. Kenosha Public Museum mural showing southwest mound from the residential district

through time, perhaps as the southwest mound itself was rebuilt and expanded. In the 1950s, archaeologists supervised the bulldozer removal of the topsoil over the southern part of this enclosure to rebuild the great southwest mound. This exposed bastions and walls that Barrett had found earlier, as well as other lines of posts, large storage pits, and several burials near the wall, including one individual without a head.

It could be that the enclosure simply functioned as an extra defense for the adjacent chiefly southwest mound. However, it enclosed the highest ridge of the site and such elevations would have had great spiritual significance in a Mississippian town plan. It is more likely that this space was reserved for special rituals and activities. Since it was physically linked to the great southwest mound, we infer that activities within the southwest enclosure were intimately associated with the elite who used or lived on the southwest mound. In 2003, the Wisconsin Historical Society's Office of the State Archaeologist and the firm Earth Information Technology examined the southwest enclosure area using electromagnetic conductivity technology. This remote sensing technique measures subsurface soil differences without disturbing the land. It has been used elsewhere to locate underground anomalies that represent soil disturbances associated with ancient building and other activities without massive excavations. Results of the survey suggest that below-surface remnants of some large features that Lapham mapped still exist. (Figure 4.23) What activities they reflect will be a matter of future research, and needless to say, the mystery of the southwest enclosure will one day be solved.

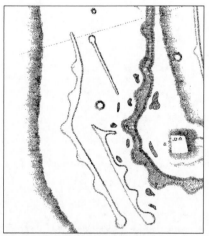

Figure 4.23. Detail of Lapham map from *Antiquities of Wisconsin* showing features in the area of the southwest enclosure as they appeared in 1855

OUTSIDE OF THE TOWN

Activities of the Aztalan and other Indian people extended beyond the walls of the town and formed a large cultural landscape around the site that bears on the life and history of the site itself. This cultural landscape includes mounds, enclosures, and the agricultural fields.

The Agricultural Fields

A large level stretch of fertile river terrace lies just north of the town and this is presumed to be the place where the people of Aztalan grew crops of corn and squash. One map produced by Nathaniel Hyer shows about forty-five acres that appear to be Indian agricultural fields as marked by blocks of ridges, a characteristic way that many Indians formed their fields. Indian farmers hoed dirt into rows of long broad ridges and planted the crops on top of the ridges. This ridged field agricultural technique is well documented and extends back one thousand years in Wisconsin. Modern farming obliterated all surface evidence of the ancient fields. Limited archaeological testing in this area by Michigan State University, under the direction of Goldstein, has not yet found evidence of the fields, but has located apparent ceremonial fires.

This area may not have been the only place where crops were grown. Archaeological surveys found fragments of stone hoes to the southwest of town, in a level area largely devoid of other cultural material and features, suggesting that this area was also cultivated. Farther south, Michigan State University archaeologists found ancient hoe fragments in an area that had not been disturbed by modern plowing. Excavations here found a portion of a house and a hearth, along with Late Woodland and Mississippian artifacts.

Mounds and Mound Groups

From early maps of the site, it is clear that the town was surrounded by earthen conical mounds of various sizes. Lapham's map shows many mounds extending along a northeast-trending ridge from the southwest enclosure, and several other mounds around the northwest end of the town. All of these mounds have been obliterated by modern farming so nothing is known about them. It is not even certain if they are associated with the town of Aztalan since the burial mound-building Woodland people lived in the region for eight hundred years prior to the founding of Aztalan. On the other hand, the mounds could well be burial places for some Late Woodland people living with the Mississippians, carrying out their own burial customs.

Three other groups of conical mounds occupied the ridge and slope northwest of the site, but again, we do not know if all of these mounds had a connection to the Mississippian town of Aztalan. However, one line of mounds, the Ceremonial Post Mound Group, described below, may represent activities related to Aztalan ceremonial life.

GREENWOOD MOUND GROUP

The westernmost mound group, called the Greenwood Mound Group, generally follows the northeast-southwest orientation of a ridge west of the present county highway. Barrett's early twentieth-century exploration revealed burial pits under some mounds containing cremated human remains and one bundle of bones. He did not find artifacts that would help place the mounds in time, so their connection to Aztalan is uncertain. Cremation and the bundling of selected bones for burial were among the mortuary rituals practiced at Aztalan but both of these customs also have great antiquity. Due to years of farming and the archaeological excavations, the Greenwood Group is no longer visible except in aerial photographs that clearly show "soil shadows" where they were once located (Figure 4.24).

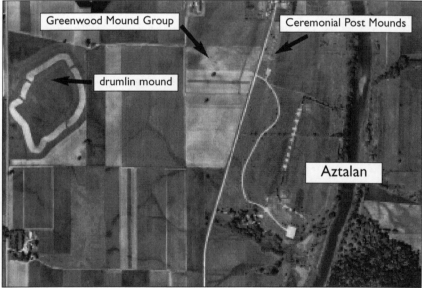

Figure 4.24. 1963 aerial photo showing soil shadows of the Greenwood Mound Group, Ceremonial Post Mounds, and former location of a drumlin mound

THE CEREMONIAL POST MOUNDS AND "PRINCESS BURIAL"

The longest line of conical mounds is the mysterious and unique Ceremonial Post Mound Group. This group is arranged in a northeast orientation following a high ridge that partly overlooks the ancient agricultural fields. Lapham's map shows thirty mounds in this line, but only nine remain today (Figure 4.25). Many of these mounds were quite large and, at one location, two large mounds are joined.

Figure 4.25. Existing Ceremonial Post mounds at Aztalan

Digging by Lapham and Barrett found that at least six of these mounds covered the locations of large and presumably very high wooden ceremonial posts, nearly two feet in diameter. These posts had been set into large pits about five feet deep packed with rock and soil (Figures 4.26a, b, c, and d). The posts had been removed prior to the construction of the mounds, but in one case a broken base of a wooden post remained in the hole. One post had been placed next to a huge boulder. Layers of charcoal and ash, and formal fireplaces around some of the post pits suggest that people conducted rituals at these places prior to burial under mounds. No artifacts, however, have been found.

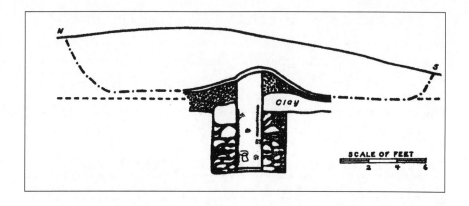

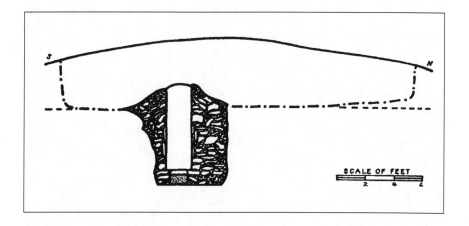

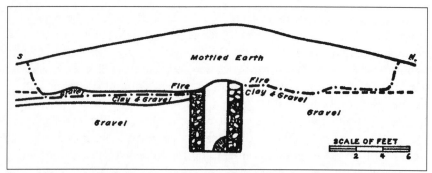

Figure 4.26a, b, and c. Profile drawings of Ceremonial Post mounds from Barrett's *Ancient Aztalan*

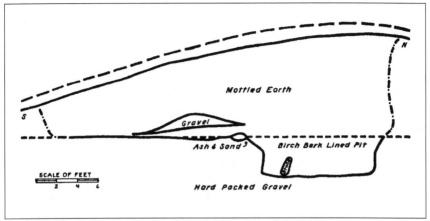

Figure 4.26d. Profile drawing of rock burial mound from Barrett's *Ancient Aztalan*

Based on many historical references to this practice, Barrett hypothe-
sized that these posts were raised during the annual Green Corn ceremonies.
The post locations overlooked the ancient agricultural fields, lending some
weight to this interpretation, but historical accounts of other Mississippian
towns place the Green Corn ceremonial posts inside the towns or village
plazas. Further, the Mississippians and other Native Americans erected ceremonial posts for many other reasons, including marking astronomical events.
At Cahokia, for example, large posts formed solar calendars such as the
famous "woodhenge." Cahokia residents also erected two large ceremonial
posts, later removed and covered by mounds, to initiate the complex and
long-term construction of the Mound 72 burial complex.[21] In the 1980s,
the Madison Astronomical Society and University of Wisconsin–Madison
civil engineering professor James Scherz identified several alignments of various features both in and outside of the town of Aztalan that they believe
may have been important solar and lunar observation points.[22]However the
posts were used at Aztalan, it is obvious that they were important to the
beliefs of the people who erected them—so important that their original
locations were accorded a mound usually reserved for human beings.

The special and sacred quality of the Ceremonial Post group is also evident from several other interesting discoveries. Below another mound in this
line, Barrett found a large pit lined with birch bark and enclosing a large
rock, also apparently wrapped in bark. For many Indian people, certain rocks
and boulders have special supernatural meaning and offerings are frequently
left at their locations. Rocks, presumably sacred, occasionally have been

found in burial mounds of the Woodland people of the area, including effigy mounds. We will probably never know what this rock meant to Aztalan people.

Certainly the most intriguing mound in this group is the one at the north end of the line that can still be viewed in back of the old settler's church in the heart of the pioneer village (Figure 4.27). This mound contained the only identified human burial in this unusual mound group. This was a young woman, wrapped in bands of many thousands of shell beads, that Barrett called the "princess." Although young, the woman had suffered from slight curvature of the spine, apparently caused by an arthritic condition. The elaborate beaded shroud, that included some seashell beads, is reminiscent of the Mound 72 chief's burial at Cahokia, laid on a beaded platform in the shape of a bird. Barrett found no other artifacts that could be used to date the burial, but such elaborately beaded burials are not known for the indigenous Woodland people.

Figure 4.27. The "princess" mound

Although called a "princess," the actual status of this young woman is unknown. She could be a part of the chiefly lineage. Since the burial is the first, or last, mound in the long line of mostly ceremonial post mounds, her death and burial may have been associated with the beginning or ending of the rituals associated with the ceremonial post line. Needless to say, the location of her burial is a major clue that may one day solve the mystery of her status and this mysterious mound group in general.

Early maps of Aztalan by Lapham and Hyer show a third line of conical mounds on the slope just below the Ceremonial Post Mound Group and running parallel to it. Lapham mapped fourteen mounds and they appear to have been smaller than those above it. Unfortunately, nineteenth-century plowing destroyed these mounds so there are no details regarding their function.

DRUMLIN MOUNDS

West of the three mound lines, another mound may be linked to Aztalan. On the top of a very high hill, possibly a glacial feature, one-half mile away from the ancient town, was a lone conical mound excavated by Barrett. It was not a human burial mound, but like the marker mounds, covered a deep pit, with slabs of rock mistakenly called pipestone by Barrett. Recent examinations of the material identify it as burned limestone.[23] This may have been the location of another ceremonial post, an observation point, or even some type of astronomical marker, but as yet its connection to Aztalan is uncertain.

A second high hill, called a glacial drumlin, one mile north of the town, may have also functioned as an observation or signal point. On top of this hill there is a small flat-topped mound that overlooks the Crawfish River, giving a clear view upstream. It is within eyesight of Aztalan and some have speculated that it was used to signal approaching danger to the town. Curiously, an effigy mound in the shape of either a headless human being or a bird was once located near the base of the north slope of the drumlin, indicating that this was also a place used by the Late Woodland effigy mound people.

East Side of the River

Increase A. Lapham, Theodore H. Lewis, and Samuel A. Barrett also described or mapped cultural features on the east side of the Crawfish River, opposite the ancient town of Aztalan. Of particular interest is a large effigy mound mapped by Barrett, and a nearby rectangular "enclosure" containing other mounds mapped by both Lewis and Barrett, but no longer clearly visible. Modern soil analysis of the area, conducted by Michigan State

University under the direction of Goldstein, provides an alternative explanation—the enclosure may have been remnants of other effigy mounds. Other conical mounds are located nearby.

Goldstein also led archaeological surveys over an extensive area on the east side of the river to determine to what extent the Native Americans used this area. The archaeologists found evidence of some use by Mississippians but many of the artifacts are Late Woodland, including sherds of Madison ware pottery made by the effigy mound builders. They also examined an earthen embankment along the river that Lapham mapped in the 1850s, and indeed found it to be the probable result of human activity. Like many of the cultural features surrounding Aztalan, the function and dating of this feature remain a mystery to be solved by future research. As well, Dr. Scherz and the Madison Astronomical Society have identified a winter solstice alignment connecting features on the east side of the river to the great southwest platform mound.

FIVE

Life at Aztalan

The physical layout and principal features of the town, along with knowledge of Mississippian culture, tell us much about the people that lived in Aztalan. In addition, tens of thousands of artifacts painstakingly recovered by archaeologists through the decades provide further and detailed insights that help reconstruct everyday life, and also link the town to both Mississippian and indigenous Woodland people of the Upper Midwest. Although this picture of life at Aztalan is incomplete, it is being filled in as new discoveries are made and archaeologists continue to analyze artifacts and information recovered in previous years.

PEOPLE AND POTTERY

Broken pieces of pottery form the largest and most common class of artifacts found at the site, representing several thousand individual vessels.[1] These tell us the most about the origins and social composition of the people themselves. Although we characterize Aztalan as a Mississippian site, it is important to emphasize that much of the pottery is in fact from what probably was a different ethnic group—people that archaeologists call Late Woodland. These people may have been indigenous to the area, or may have migrated from the south like the Mississippians, or both. The origin of people living with the Mississippians is a matter of continuing research.

Nonetheless, the Mississippian pottery assemblage at Aztalan is unparalleled in Wisconsin in sheer numbers and the variety of forms (Figures 5.1, 5.2, and 5.3). Further, most of the styles and forms are visually indistinguishable from those at Cahokia itself. Among the many forms are dippers, plates, pans, bottles, bowls, jars, and pots of various sizes and styles. On some vessels, Native pottery makers applied a thin film in colors of buff and black and decorated many bowls and pots with characteristic Mississippian designs such as chevrons and interlocking scrolls. Several styles of bowls that were used for water featured molded effigy heads of waterfowl and other birds, a type of vessel found at many other Mississippian communities. Some of the pottery, like Ramey Incised, was apparently made for ceremonial occasions.

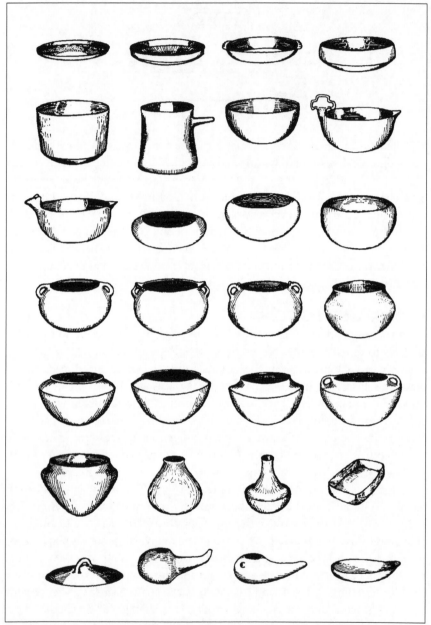

Figure 5.1. Drawing of different Mississippian pottery forms found at Aztalan, adopted from Barrett's *Ancient Aztalan*

The Mississippian pottery at Cahokia, Aztalan, and elsewhere is so well made that some believe that these societies had pottery-making specialists. Among Aztalan artifacts are specialized tools used to form and smooth pot interiors.

Figure 5.2. Reconstructed Mississippian pot

Figure 5.3. Ceramic gourd dipper

THE AZTALAN DIET

The remains of food and food-related artifacts lead us to conclude that the people of Aztalan enjoyed a well-balanced and nourishing diet consisting primarily of corn, venison, and fish, and supplemented by a variety of other seasonally available foods.[2]

The remains of deer are especially plentiful and account for the vast majority of animal remains found at the town. Fish speared at the fish dam and caught by other means included catfish, bass, buffalo fish, pike, drum, and gar. Other animals routinely taken for food included small mammals, clams, waterfowl, and the now extinct passenger pigeon.

Analysis of food remains excavated from the layers of the "town dump" along the river by the University of Wisconsin-Milwaukee in the 1980s shows there was some change in the animal protein part of the Aztalan diet through time; the people used more river resources, such as fish and clams.[3] However, agriculture formed the base of the Aztalan diet. Archaeologists have found burned corncobs and kernels as well as squash seeds throughout the site. Wild foods, such as nuts, berries, and a variety of seeds also contributed to the vegetable diet. These foods were eaten fresh, and also ground into meal with stone pestles.

TOOLS AND ECONOMIC ACTIVITIES

The Aztalan people crafted simple and some beautifully made tools from materials found around them: stone, bone, and almost certainly wood. Stone toolmakers used chert, an easily worked rock, for many common tools such as arrowheads, scraping tools, drills, and knives. The limestone formations of southern Wisconsin bear several forms of chert. Basalt and other hard rock found in glacial deposits made good material for axes needed for construction of Aztalan's formidable walls and many other purposes. Smaller ungrooved versions of these axes, called celts, were used in woodworking. Animals not only provided food—bone and antlers served as raw material for tools like needles, awls, points of various types, and tools to soften the skins of deer and other animals for use in garments (Figures 5.4a, b, c, and d).

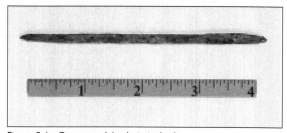

Figure 5.4a. Copper awl (scale in inches)

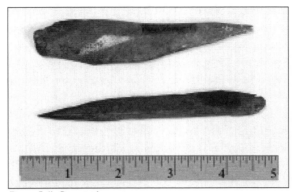

Figure 5.4b. Bone awls

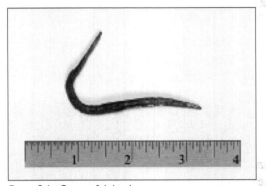

Figure 5.4c. Copper fish hook

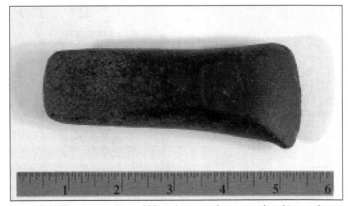

Figure 5.4d. The stone celt would have been used as a woodworking tool.

The Indian farmers raised crops by tilling the soil with stone hoes and clam shells (Figures 5.5 and 5.6). These same tools were probably used to help build the earthen platform mounds and in other construction in the town. The material for the hoes, however, appears imported. Most stone hoe blades found at Aztalan are of a rock called Mill Creek chert imported from southern Illinois, near the city of Cahokia itself. Mill Creek is found in a natural tabular or flat form making it easier to produce large flat stone tools. This chert appears to have been used for hoe production at Cahokia. Aztalan farmers also crafted other hoe blades from the thick shells of large clam species and these also came from elsewhere. Analysis of Aztalan clam shell hoes by University of Wisconsin–La Crosse professor James Theler identified two main species of freshwater mussel, *Megalonaias nervosa* and *Amblema plicata plicata,* whose ranges did not extend to the Crawfish or Rock Rivers until modern times. Sources would have been the Mississippi River, one hundred miles away, or possibly the Illinois River.[4]

Figure 5.5. Stone hoe

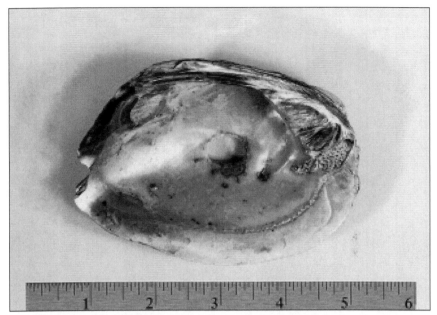

Figure 5.6. Clam shell hoe, the shell would have been hafted to a wooden handle.

The Aztalan fishermen used bone spears and even copper and bone fish-hooks. They probably also used nets since the technology was available and widespread at the time. Aztalan hunters and warriors used the bow and arrow, introduced into the Midwest about AD 500 (Figure 5.7). They tipped their arrows with small triangular stone points. Many arrowheads found at Aztalan, called Cahokia points, are of a typical Mississippian style, bearing two or three notches for hafting. Many others are simple unnotched trian-gular forms widely favored by many peoples of the region and also used by the Mississippians. The notched Cahokia points are mostly made of cherts found in the area, but the unnotched arrowheads are frequently made of Hixton Silicified Sandstone, only found in west-central Wisconsin. The pri-mary quarries for Hixton Silicified Sandstone are at a small mountain, called Silver Mound, just outside of Hixton, Wisconsin. Midwestern Native Americans used and traded this beautiful golden and reddish-hued rock for twelve thousand years. Just what made this rock so desirable for so long is unknown. But there are some clues. Some pictographs or rock paintings at and near the quarries depict bird imagery, and in one case, on Hixton deposits in the near vicinity of the quarries, there is a thunderbird rendered in Native American artistic tradition. This, combined with the fact that the

Figure 5.7. Aztalan arrow points, notched and unnotched. The center point is made of quartz.

rock hues capture the colors of the sun, could mean that the use of the material called upon the powers of the celestial world. Significantly, among the offerings in Cahokia's Mound 72, which included the famous beaded birdman, was a cache of Hixton arrowheads made in Mississippian fashion.

The difference between the stone used to make the notched Mississippian-style arrowheads and the unnotched arrowheads may reflect the preferences of the two different people living at the site. However, it may also indicate that different arrowheads were used for different activities. Some archaeologists who have studied the matter suggest that the unnotched points of the time were made for war. Supported by historical accounts and archaeological evidence, they reason that notching made for securely hafted points needed for hunting but that the unnotched war points would more easily detach from the shaft and remain in the wound of the

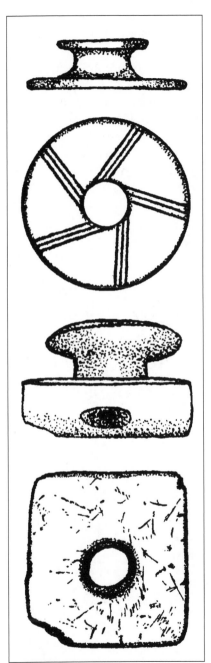

Figure 5.8. Drawings of earspools including a decorated one as illustrated in Barrett's *Ancient Aztalan*

enemy when the arrow shaft was pulled out.[5] If true, it would explain why the unnotched war arrows were made from a special stone that may have given the warrior supernatural aid in life and death situations.

PERSONAL APPEARANCE

The Aztalan people, especially those from elite families, often adorned themselves with objects made from special materials that held symbolic meaning or denoted a special status. These included shell and copper beads; clay and stone earspools or plugs that fit into large holes made in the earlobe; stone pendants; and shell pendants made from large seashells like whelks from the Gulf of Mexico or Atlantic Coast. The earspools and whelk pendants are intimately linked with the Mississippians and are often depicted in Mississippian art where they are worn by leaders, warriors, or religious specialists. One earspool found at Aztalan by an early farmer is decorated with spiraling lines, possibly a version of the classic Mississippian circle and cross sun symbol (Figure 5.8). About a dozen Aztalan earspools were made from a purple Baraboo pipestone found only in the Baraboo Hills about sixty miles northwest of Aztalan, and one was made from a red Minnesota pipestone called catlinite.[6]

Among the rare and highly important ornaments found at Aztalan are two copper long-nosed god maskettes (Figure 5.9a and b). This type of ornament, a small human face that once bore a long nose, was worn as an earring and is linked by some archaeologists to the Native American culture hero, Red Horn, or "He Who Wears Human Heads As Earrings." Similar maskettes of copper and seashell have been found in towns and villages throughout the area of Mississippian influence extending from Wisconsin to Florida. Mississippian art depicts warriors and high status people wearing these distinctive objects thought to be somehow associated with long-distance trade and the ritual identification of Red Horn who had been magically brought back to life.[7]

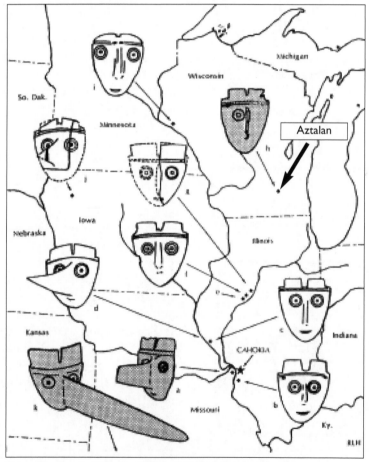

Figure 5.9a. Drawings of god maskettes from the Mississippian region

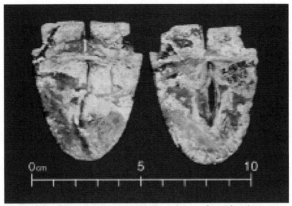

Figure 5.9b. Copper long-nosed god maskettes from Aztalan

Much clothing would have been made from deer and other animal skins. But the Mississippians also wove complex textiles from plant fibers. Chandler Rowe found a piece of such a textile with one of the skeletons in the northwest platform mound mortuary house during his 1950s excavations.[8] One fragment of a clay figurine found by Barrett at Aztalan depicts an individual wearing a typical Mississippian skirt that may have been made of textile. This figurine fragment provides a firsthand glimpse of how the Aztalan people dressed (Figure 5.10).

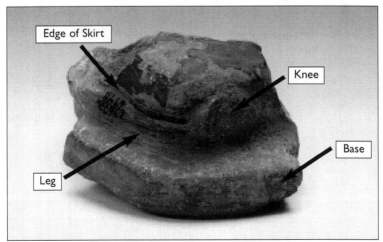

Figure 5.10. Fragmentary base of clay Aztalan figurine depicting a figure, probably a woman, sitting on legs—a characteristic Mississippian figurine pose. Note knee, leg, and section of skirt.

CEREMONIAL LIFE

The people of Aztalan, like other Indian societies, enjoyed a rich ceremonial life that guided all activities and marked special events. There would have been many rituals, ceremonies, and dances held for special clan activities; curing and medicine; marking rites-of-passage; bringing success to hunts, agriculture, and warfare; and for death. Religious specialists, variously called shamans, medicine men, or priests, conducted or led rituals and ceremonies. The chief of the town himself would have been viewed more as a religious leader rather than a purely political head.

The fragmentary clay figurine found at Aztalan, noted above, provides a direct link to Cahokia and Mississippian art and symbolism. It is part of Barrett's archaeological collection from the site but is described as a possible frog in his 1933 *Ancient Aztalan* publication. It is a figurine base depicting a kneeling figure, sitting on its legs, and wearing a short skirt. There appears to be no garment on the upper torso. Remnants of red paint adhere to the base and the skirt has an orange hue. The dress of the individual identifies it as a probable female based on comparison to other Mississippian figurines, including those found in the Cahokia area. The sitting posture of the figure is similar to the red stone Keller figurine from the BBB Motor site near Cahokia, and a large, marble female figure from the later Mississippian site of Etowah in Georgia (Figures 5.11 and 5.12).[9] Based on historical accounts and some archaeological evidence, Mississippian art specialists believe that these figurines are representations of deities or ancestors and were kept in temples. Female figurines are associated with fertility symbols such as plants (corn, gourds, vines), plant-grinding implements, and serpents of the watery, hence fertile, underworld. One authority, Thomas Emerson of the University of Illinois at Urbana-Champaign, believes that the female figurines embody earth mother and corn maiden concepts.[10]

The Aztalan figurine could have been broken in any number of ways, considering it is clay. However, archaeologists found several female figurines made from a red stone called "fireclay" on Cahokia-area temple sites that had been deliberately smashed and discarded. It may be that such destruction accompanied fertility-oriented new life rituals that involved production of new symbols and discarding the old.

Almost certainly, the Aztalan people did indeed celebrate the new agricultural year with a new life festival called the Green Corn ceremony, as was done elsewhere in the Mississippian world.[11] Marking the new agricultural year, it was the central ceremonial event. Mississippian people began this several-day religious festival when the first corn ripened. Specialists made clay

Figure 5.11. Stone Keller Figurine depicting sitting woman grinding corn from the BBB Motor Site in Illinois

Figure 5.12. Large marble figure of sitting woman from the Etowah site in Georgia

vessels for the ritual consumption of cleansing medicines and the plazas were swept clean. People fasted before the ceremonies and were prohibited from eating corn until the ceremonies were completed. Temple priests extinguished and rekindled the sacred fire in a ritual symbolizing new life. The townspeople lighted new household fires from the sacred fire.

Somewhere at Aztalan, probably in the plaza, men played the ceremonial chunkey game. Many of the distinctive granite chunkey stones, typically only three to four inches in diameter, have been found at Aztalan (Figure 5.13). We cannot say whether the town competed with other people in the region, but through the years, chunkey stones, often called "discoidals," have been discovered in several places in Wisconsin where there is evidence of Mississippian influence. The following narrative of

Figure 5.13. Chunkey stone from Aztalan

the chunkey game is taken from an eighteenth-century French account of the Natchez and describes how the game may have been played at Aztalan:

> *Only two play this game, and each has a pole of the same kind. They have a flat stone shaped like a wheel, beveled on both sides like the wheel of the game of Siam. But it is only 3 inches in diameter and an inch thick. The first throws his stick and rolls the stone at the same time. The skill of the player consists in managing so that the stone touches the pole or stops very close to it. The second throws his pole the instant the stone begins to roll. The one whose pole is nearest the stone scores a point and has the right to throw the stone. The men become very much fatigued over the game I just described, because they run after their poles as if by running they could guide them in accordance with their wishes.*[12]

TRADE AND OUTSIDE RELATIONS

The sources of artifacts and raw materials tell us much about Aztalan's relationships with the outside world and demonstrate that, despite its defensive posture, the town was not cut off from the rest of the world. Most notably, there was contact with Cahokia and its trade networks as indicated by the presence of Cahokia-made pottery, seashell pendants, and stone hoes made from southern Illinois stone. It is unlikely that the Mississippians would have brought all of this material, used for many generations, in one brief migration. Whether the Aztalan people acquired these items directly or through intermediate trading partners is yet to be determined.

While Aztalan stone craftsman mostly used chert and other rock found in the vicinity of the town, they directly acquired or traded for other special stone and metals from elsewhere in the region. As noted above, this included Baraboo pipestone, Hixton Silicified Sandstone from west-central Wisconsin, pipestone from Minnesota, and possibly copper from northern Michigan. Other items brought to the town from quite some distance were the large thick shells of several species of clam, common to the Mississippi and Illinois Rivers, which were used as hoes.

Some of the material may have been acquired through a network of trade intermediaries. That Aztalan maintained peaceful relationships with some close neighbors is clear from the many Late Woodland people that lived at the town itself. Additional evidence for some peaceful relations is that Late Woodland people also lived in nearby camps or villages that lacked fortifications and these sites contained a few Mississippian trade items such as pottery and arrowheads intermixed with the village debris.[13]

The people of Aztalan also may have acquired material from other Mississippian centers. The Trempealeau Mound complex and nearby Mississippian sites on the Mississippi River, for example, are located fairly close to the Hixton Silicified Sandstone or Hixton quarries. Hixton chipping debris found at Aztalan indicates that the material was brought to the town in roughed-out, unfinished forms, rather than as blocks of raw material.[14]

The people of Aztalan also used copper for tools and other objects. The source for this metal is thought to be northern Michigan where extensive pre-Columbian quarries are still visible on the landscape. Melvin Fowler believes that Aztalan's location with access to both the Mississippi River and northern Michigan (over portages via the Fox River and Wisconsin Rivers), put Aztalan on a strategic point in the trade or movement of copper between the quarries and the rest of the Mississippian world, including Cahokia.[15] Significantly in this light, the two long-nosed god maskettes found at Aztalan, thought by some to symbolize trade relationships, are made from copper. On other northern Mississippian sites, they are made from seashell. We should point out, however, that copper is not overly abundant at Aztalan, and what there is could be from "float copper" brought down by glaciers and deposited in chunks in this region. Float copper is still found in the area.

WARFARE

Warfare was a part of Mississippian life as it was for complex societies throughout the world at the time. Warfare is a major theme in Mississippian art and there appears to have been a formal warrior society among the Mississippians, complete with standardized dress and body decoration. There is compelling evidence that Aztalan existed in an atmosphere of warfare, as did other Mississippian and other midwestern communities of the period. Foremost, it is the most heavily fortified community known in a region of many contemporaneous fortified Native American villages. Additionally, there is some skeletal evidence of violence: an arrow killed or wounded at least one individual at the site and other skulls show evidence of massive blows.[16]

If Aztalan engaged in warfare, who were they fighting? One possibility is the Oneota who had taken up residence on nearby Lake Koshkonong. Oneota villages here appear to span or overlap the time that the Mississippians lived at nearby Aztalan.[17] Despite the proximity of Lake Koshkonong, no Oneota pottery has been found at Aztalan, suggesting a great social distance. Archaeologist David Overstreet even theorizes that the emerging Oneota population temporarily fled from the area after the establishment of Aztalan. Others think it probable that the Oneota were shifting to defensive positions on the lake itself.[18] However, like many matters regarding the culture history of the period, the relationship of the Oneota and Aztalan is unsettled. There are also other possibilities for Aztalan enemies since alliances could have been continuously shifting during this tumultuous and unstable period. As noted, a warrior ethic, and perhaps even an institutionalized warrior society, seems to have existed among the Mississippians, and this also could have contributed to conflict as young men sought opportunities to distinguish themselves in battle.

DEATH AND BURIAL

No main cemeteries that served the general populace have yet been found at Aztalan, and perhaps do not exist. Instead, burials are in many forms and scattered throughout the site, including the residential area where people were interred near their homes. The mortuary house on the northwest mound, the "crematory" that Barrett found in the residential precinct, and the remains of many people near the southeast knoll indicate that mortuary rituals were often complex and some bodies were processed through a number of steps over a length of time. The mortuary practices for some people, including the chiefly lineage, followed a distinctive Mississippian pattern involving charnel houses as temporary repositories for the dead, the saving and bundling of some bones, and subsequent reburial. The large number of small conical mounds found around the town itself may indicate the Woodland people living at the site pursued their own burial customs. We do not yet understand the full range of mortuary practices at Aztalan, or the Mississippians in general, except that they reflect a variety of customs.

CANNIBALISM REVISITED

Early excavations at Aztalan unearthed a surprising number of scattered human bones discarded in refuse pits, fireplaces, and refuse deposits. A notable concentration was found near the southeast knoll. The bones and bone fragments found here represent all parts of the skeleton and many show clear signs of cutting, dismemberment, breaking, and charring. Some were cracked open as if to extract bone marrow, much like animal bone found at archaeological sites. Barrett and others thought these human remains represented cannibalism.

Some rare instances of true cannibalism—the consumption of human flesh for food—have indeed been reported for ancient North America and elsewhere in the ancient world,[19] but this was not the case at Aztalan. Some people here may have been the victims of violent customs associated with intense warfare documented for the Americas and elsewhere. Such customs included the taking of "trophy" heads, hands, and other body parts from dead enemies, *ritual* consumption of body parts, and the torture, dismemberment, and burning of prisoners.[20]

Moreover, one modern analysis suggests that the pattern at Aztalan is mainly (but not exclusively) the by-product of well-documented Mississippian funerary customs.[21] As noted previously, the Mississippians practiced complex funerary rituals that included dismemberment, bone processing and bundling, and reburial of some bones, as well as cremation. During these rituals some bone, notably skulls, were saved for ancestor veneration, and conversely some bone appears to have been discarded. The saving, bundling, and eventual reburial of bones was not unique to the Mississippians and was a common practice for people of North America, stretching far back into antiquity. Even in more recent times, some groups, such as the Huron, conducted a periodic "Feast of the Dead" ceremony in which residents of related villages would disinter their ancestors and kin, clean the bones, and rebury them in a common tribal grave pit.[22] What is unusual about Aztalan as compared to other period sites, however, is that so much fragmentary broken and cut human bone was discarded. This is another one of the Aztalan mysteries that needs to be solved.

ABANDONMENT

No one yet knows why the Indian people left Aztalan. Perhaps the demise of Cahokia cut it off from its parent community. If Aztalan functioned as a trading outpost, it would simply have lost its reason to exist. Alternately, trouble at the Mississippian frontier may have been a harbinger of Cahokia's collapse. After AD 1200–1300 in Wisconsin, large populations of Oneota dominated many parts of the region, supported by corn agriculture, and sometimes, fortified villages. The cultural tradition known as Late Woodland had disappeared. The Mississippians and their allies at Aztalan therefore could have been ultimately driven out by the emerging Oneota. As with ancient Rome, the fate of Cahokia may have been sealed by people of the frontiers. Or perhaps the Aztalan community dispersed due to climate change; a paleoclimate model suggests there was a lengthy decrease in precipitation that could have affected local food supplies in this region.

Whatever the case, a long life would not be expected for such a town. Cahokia aside, Native American towns and villages typically moved after several generations due to such practical factors as depletion of firewood in the area and soil exhaustion. Studies of later Mississippian towns in Tennessee estimate that towns lasted between 50 and 150 years before soil exhaustion forced dispersal or relocation.[23] Aztalan certainly must have faced the same problems, but the town did not relocate—it vanished.

In the nineteenth century, settlers found the burned remains of Aztalan and the huge ridges of clay and dirt that represented its walls. It is possible that the burning of Aztalan took place at abandonment. On the other hand, frequent natural fires that burned over the prairies of the area could have consumed the town as clay from the walls slumped through time, exposing the dried timber beneath.

After abandonment by the Mississippians, Wisconsin Indians used Aztalan one other time. East of the southeast knoll, Barrett discovered a camp or small village dated to the eighteenth or early nineteenth century as indicated by the presence of trade items such as iron knives, fishhooks, portions of brass kettles, gunflints, and musket parts. A sketch map made by Increase Lapham in 1850 shows corn hills on the former Aztalan residential area, an agricultural method used by Native Americans in the historic period.[24] At this time, the Ho-Chunk or Winnebago lived in the upper Rock River region and several families continued to use the area near Aztalan for quite some time after white settlement began.[25] The camp or village that Barrett found was located immediately adjacent to the Aztalan fish dam, so it is likely that these most recent residents of Aztalan used and maintained this structure, as they did on nearby rivers during the same period. We now wonder if these people told stories of the once great town as they lived among its ruins.

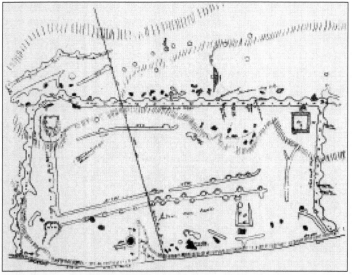

Figure 5.14. A map sketched by Increase Lapham in 1850 showing location of corn hills (lower center)

SIX

Aztalan State Park

It is appropriate that Wisconsin should have at least one park that features as the primary attraction the prehistory of the state.

—W. C. McKern, Milwaukee Public Museum, 1946[1]

Standing at the quiet center of Aztalan State Park today, one has little trouble imagining the past. Except for a small kiosk on the southeast knoll, a few small signs, and small segments of reconstructed stockade, there is hardly a modern structure in sight. Even restrooms are discretely hidden from view along a tree line. Hawks routinely crisscross the parkland skies searching for prey on the same territory where falcon-warriors once kept watch. The serenity of the place is the result of long preservation efforts by many individuals, organizations, and institutions.

Figure 6.1. Aztalan has been designated as a National Landmark and is listed on the National Register of Historic Places. Visitors to Aztalan can enjoy quiet walks enhanced by self-guided tour brochures and interpretive signs.

The significance of Aztalan to Wisconsin history and the need to pre-serve the remarkable site was recognized from the very start. Nathaniel F. Hyer, who in 1837 brought Aztalan to public attention, wrote in the *Milwaukee Advertiser* of his determination to "preserve these ruins from ruin" in the face of the settlement that he predicted would take place in the area.[2] There is also a story of an unsuccessful effort made the following year to withdraw the land from public sale. In 1855, Lapham took up the cause for preservation in *The Antiquities of Wisconsin,* noting that a wheat crop was already growing on the great south wall of the ancient town.[3]

Settlement did creep west. Everywhere newly arrived settlers cleared forests and drained swamps, preparing the land for cultivation. In the mid-nineteenth century, farmers returned to Aztalan, this time carting away the burned remnants of Aztalan's clay walls, plowing down mounds, and plant-ing modern fields of corn over the ancient town. Relic hunters also had their field day. Eventually, many of the surface features of the town, so carefully mapped by Lapham, disappeared.

Excavations by the Milwaukee Public Museum renewed interest in preservation in the 1920s. The Wisconsin Archeological Society and Wisconsin Historical Society formed a "Save Aztalan" committee, spear-headed by Publius Lawson, an industrialist from Menasha. In 1928, with the support of many organizations and individuals, even money collected by local school children, the Wisconsin Archeological Society raised sufficient funds to purchase land around the eight surviving ceremonial post mounds overlooking the ancient town. It became a popular local park.

After the Great Depression, pleas were made to the National Park Service to make Aztalan a national park. The National Park Service made a favorable assessment, especially if the site could be reconstructed, but for economic reasons this never materialized.[4] However, stimulated by activities of the Wisconsin Archeological Society, the Wisconsin Historical Society, and the Lake Mills-Aztalan Historical Society (formed in 1941), the Wisconsin legislature directed the State Planning Board to study Aztalan as a possible state park. Authorized by the legislature, the State Conservation Commission purchased Aztalan in 1948 on behalf of the state of Wisconsin. The state purchased a total of 120 acres surrounding the site, encompassing the small earlier park. In 1952, Aztalan State Park opened, operated by the Department of Conservation, now the Wisconsin Department of Natural Resources. That year also witnessed the continuation of major archaeological excavations by the Wisconsin Archaeological Survey—the first major study of the site since Barrett published *Ancient Aztalan.*

Recognition of the importance of the site led to its listing as a National Landmark in 1964 by the U.S. Department of Interior and subsequently it became one of the first archaeological sites in Wisconsin placed on the National Register of Historic Places. The Wisconsin Historical Society led another period of archaeological investigations during an attempt by the state to create interpretation facilities at the park. However, lack of funding for park staff that could guard reconstructions and outdoor exhibits led to the destruction of these by vandals.

Lack of funding continued to plague the state and the park was threatened with closure. In 1981, the Department of Natural Resources divested itself of several other state archaeological properties. Lizard Mounds Park, the site of a unique effigy mound group, for example, was turned over to local authorities. In the case of Aztalan, however, the local township stepped up with the offer to maintain the site if it stayed in state hands. For many years the people of Aztalan Township maintained the park, keeping it open for visitors to enjoy. Hyer would have been proud to know that over one hundred and fifty years later, the people of his township were still determined "to preserve these ruins from ruin."

The Historic Sites Task Force created in the late 1980s began to change the fortunes of the park. Together, the Wisconsin Historical Society and Department of Natural Resources focused on Aztalan and some other state historic sites to enhance their futures. The task force noted that Aztalan was a special concern because of its potential for research, public interpretation, and tourism: "Housing one of the largest and significant archaeological treasures in the state of Wisconsin, Aztalan contains enormous historical and cultural value for Wisconsin citizens." [5] As a result of task force recommendations, the first permanent employee for the park was hired.

Public interest in Native American history and archaeology grew dramatically at the end of the twentieth century and also added to renewed interest in Aztalan State Park. Archaeologists returned to the site, further stimulating public interest in Aztalan and the Mississippians. Each year, tens of thousands of people visited the park despite lack of advertising and interpretation. A Friends of Aztalan State Park group formed in 1994 to assist the Department of Natural Resources with fundraising, tours and other park programs, and an advisory board of experts was created to guide the park in research matters.

Between 1997 and 2002, the Department of Natural Resources developed the first long-term plan with input from archaeologists, Native American nations, and the public at large. As a part of this process, Lynne

Figures 6.2a and b. Aztalan State Park attracts thousands of visitors and schoolchildren for special tours and programs. Art Shogonee (Potawatomi/Menominee) demonstrates Native American pow-wow dances during a special program at Aztalan.

Goldstein and students at Michigan State University assembled all information pertaining to the site, producing base maps that show the significant features and the extent of previous archaeological work.[6] Among other things,
the state master plan recommends building an interpretive center so that the
dramatic story of Aztalan can be told. In 2004, proposed budget cuts forced
the Department of Natural Resources to again consider eliminating funding
to the park, but local legislators and an outpouring of public support con-
vinced lawmakers to continue modest state support. Adequate funding for
the state park remains a problem, but park supporters are confident that
increasing public interest in the story of Aztalan will guarantee its accessibil-
ity for generations to come.

At Aztalan, limited archaeological work also continues, but with
renewed caution and respect. As with modern communities, Aztalan includes
graves and remains of the many people that lived there over several generations. Wisconsin law now protects such gravesites as it does for ancient and
modern tombs throughout the state. A sense of respect for the lives and resting places of the ancient Indian inhabitants should also accompany visitors as
they tour the fascinating site.

THE FUTURE

The name Aztalan poignantly reminds us of a time when Euro Americans
refused to acknowledge that the native population was capable of such won-
ders or even that North American Indians had a deep history that connected them to the land. The name also now symbolizes a fascinating and important time in Native American history that molded much of what was to come
later. Indeed, the legacy of the Mississippians and Woodland people can be
found around us today in the form of corn agriculture. Wisconsin still derives
its identity from this crop, and it appears prominently on the state quarter
issued in 2004. In this light, Aztalan can be recognized as the state's first
farming town.

Through archaeological and historical work, many of the mysteries of
Aztalan have been solved. However, many other questions remain. For
example: what lies beneath the surface in the plaza area, the mysterious
southwest enclosure, and between the platform mounds in the elite precinct?
What is the meaning of the ceremonial posts overlooking the town? There
are also larger questions: Why did the Mississippians come to Aztalan and
why did they leave? What was the relationship of these people to others such
as the Late Woodland effigy mound builders and the later Oneota? What

caused the collapse of Cahokia and who are its Mississippian descendants in the Midwest? Needless to say, these questions are much on the minds of archaeologists and other scholars, and almost every year new discoveries in Wisconsin and elsewhere in North America are made that add important data. This continuous and exciting flow of new information greatly contributes to the ever-unfolding story of Aztalan, the northern outpost of the Mississippian Indians.

Notes

CHAPTER ONE

1 Nathaniel Hyer, "Ruins of the Ancient City of Aztalan," *Milwaukee Advertiser*, February, 1837. An anonymous newspaper article published in *The Prophet* in 1845, reprinted from the Greenwich (NY) *Eagle,* gave a different version for the name. Some visiting mound diggers to the site in 1839 subsequently claimed that the name came from an unidentified seventeenth-century French traveler who learned it from the traditions of unspecified Native Americans during a tour of the "great lake," presumably Michigan or Superior. The anonymous and dubious source relates that the "Aztalans" who lived at the site later burned the town and went to Mexico. The account was much later repeated and cited by Rev. Stephen Peet who does not mention Hyer's *Milwaukee Advertiser* account. See Rev. Stephen D. Peet, "Emblematic Mounds in Wisconsin; The Forms They Represent," *Wisconsin Historical Collections* 9 (1882): 40–74.

2 William T. Sterling, "A Visit to Aztalan in 1838," *The Wisconsin Archeologist* 19, no. 1 (1920): 18–19.

3 Increase A. Lapham, *The Antiquities of Wisconsin, As Surveyed and Described.* (1855; reprint with a foreword by Robert A. Birmingham and introduction by Robert P. Nurrie, Madison: University of Wisconsin Press, 2001).

4 Theodore H. Lewis, "The 'Aztalan' Enclosure Newly Described," *American Antiquarian and Oriental Journal* 16 (1894): 205–208.

5 George A. West, "The Indian Authorship of Wisconsin Antiquities," *The Wisconsin Archeologist.* O.S. 64, no. 4 (1907): 167–256.

6 Samuel A. Barrett, *Ancient Aztalan.* Bulletin of the Museum of the City of Milwaukee 13 (1933).

7 Robert Ritzenthaler, "Aztalan: Exploration and Reconstruction," *The Wisconsin Archeologist* 39 (1958).

8 Chandler W. Rowe, "A Crematorium at Aztalan," *The Wisconsin Archeologist* 39 (1958): 101–110.

9   Paul W. Parmalee, "Animal Remains from the Aztalan Site, Jefferson County, Wisconsin," *The Wisconsin Archeologist* 41, no. 1 (1960): 1–10.

10   Lynne Goldstein and Joan Freeman, "Aztalan: A Middle Mississippian Village," *The Wisconsin Archeologist* 78, nos. 1 & 2 (1997): 223–248.

11   Fred K. Stuebe, "Site Survey and Test Excavations in the Aztalan Area," *The Wisconsin Archeologist* 57, no. 4 (1976): 198–259.

12   Lynne Goldstein and John D. Richards, "Ancient Aztalan: The Cultural and Ecological Context of a Late Prehistoric Site in the Midwest," in *Cahokia and the Hinterlands: Middle Mississippian Cultures of the Midwest,* eds. Thomas E. Emerson and Barry L. Lewis (Urbana: University of Illinois Press, 1991), 193–206.

13   John D. Richards, "Ceramics and Culture at Aztalan: A Late Prehistoric Village in Southeast Wisconsin," (PhD dissertation, University of Wisconsin–Milwaukee, 1992).

14   Lynne Goldstein and Donald H. Gaff, "Recasting the Past: Examining Assumptions about Aztalan," *The Wisconsin Archeologist* 83, no. 2 (2002): 98–110.

15   Kira E. Kaufman and William F. Kean, "Archaeological Spatial Analysis at Aztalan State Park (47JE1): Using Geophysical Techniques to Interpret Prehistoric Landscape Features," *The Wisconsin Archeologist* 83 (2002): 111–112.

CHAPTER TWO

1   Timothy R. Pauketat, *Ancient Cahokia and the Mississippians* (Cambridge: University of Cambridge Press, 2004).

2   Melvin Fowler, Jerome Rose, Barbara Vander Leest, and Steven R. Ahler, *The Mound 72 Area: Dedicated and Sacred Space in Early Cahokia.* Illinois State Museum Reports of Investigations no. 54 (Springfield, Illinois: Illinois State Museum, 1999); Biloine Whiting Young and Melvin L. Fowler, *Cahokia, The Great Native American Metropolis* (Urbana: University of Illinois Press, 2000).

3   Young and Fowler, *Cahokia, The Great Native American Metropolis,* 135.

4   Young and Fowler, *Cahokia, The Great Native American Metropolis,* 149–150.

5   Le Page Du Pratz, *Histoire de la Louisiane* (Paris: De Bure, 1758).

6   Lynne Goldstein, "Mississippian Ritual as Viewed Through the Practice of Secondary Disposal of the Dead," in *Mounds, Modoc, and Mesoamerica: Papers in Honor of Melvin L. Fowler*, ed. Steven R. Ahler, Illinois State Museum Scientific Papers 28 (Springfield: Illinois State Museum, 2000), 193–207; James A. Brown, "The Cahokia Mound 72–Sub 1 Burials as Collective Representation," *The Wisconsin Archeologist* 84, nos. 1 & 2 (2003): 81–98.

7   Pauketat, *Ancient Cahokia and the Mississippians*, 90.

8   R. Barry Lewis, Charles Stout, and Cameron B. Wesson, "The Design of Mississippian Towns," in *Mississippian Towns and Sacred Places: Searching for an Architectural Grammar*, eds. R. Barry Lewis and Charles Stout (Tuscaloosa, Alabama: University of Alabama Press, 1998), 1–21.

9. Young and Fowler, *Cahokia, The Great Native American Metropolis*, 190.

10   Thomas E. Emerson, "Water, Serpents, and the Underworld: An Exploration into Cahokia Symbolism," in *The Southeastern Ceremonial Complex; Artifacts and Analysis: The Cottonlandia Conference*, ed. Patricia Galloway (Lincoln: University of Nebraska Press, 1989), 45–92.

11   Young and Fowler,*Cahokia, The Great Native American Metropolis*, 267.

12   Robert L. Hall, *Archaeology of the Soul: North American Belief and Ritual* (Urbana: University of Illinois Press, 1997), 147–151.

13   Hall, *Archaeology of the Soul*, 145–154.

14   Robert J. Salzer and Grace Rajnovich, *The Gottschall Rockshelter: An Archaeological Mystery* (St. Paul: Prairie Smoke Press, 2000).

15   John Witthoft, *Green Corn Ceremonialism in the Eastern Woodlands*, Occasional Contributions from the Museum of Anthropology of the University of Michigan 13 (Ann Arbor: University of Michigan, Museum of Anthropology, 1949).

16   Thomas E. Emerson, *Mississippian Stone Images in Illinois*, Illinois Archaeological Survey Circular 6 (Urbana: Illinois Archaeological Survey, 1982); Emerson, "Water, Serpents, and the Underworld."

17   Paul Radin, *The Winnebago Tribe* (1923; reprint, Lincoln: University of Nebraska Press, 1990).

18   Charles M. Hudson, *The Southeastern Indians* (Knoxville: University of Tennessee Press, 1976).

19   Claudia Gellam Mink, *Cahokia: City of the Sun* (Collinsville, IL: Cahokia Mounds Museum Society, 1992).

20   Emerson, "Water, Serpents, and the Underworld."

21   Witthoft, *Green Corn Ceremonialism*, 63; John R. Swanton, *Religious Beliefs and Medical Practices of the Creek Indians,* Annual Report of the Bureau of American Ethnology (Washington D.C.: Smithsonian Institution, 1928), 559.

22   Mink, *Cahokia: City of the Sun*, 58.

23   Mink, *Cahokia: City of the Sun.*

24   Warren R. Deboer, "Like a Rolling Stone: The Chunkey Game and Political Organization in Eastern North America," *Southeastern Archaeology* 12 (1993): 83–92.

25   David S. Brose, James A. Brown, and David W. Penney, *Ancient Art of the American Woodland Indians* (New York: Harry N. Abrams, Inc., 1985), 173.

26   Goldstein, "Mississippian Ritual."

27   Amy L. Ollendorf, "Changing Landscapes in the American Bottom (USA): An Interdisciplinary Investigation with an Emphasis on the Late Prehistoric and Early Historic Periods," (PhD Dissertation, University of Minnesota–Minneapolis, 1993), 175.

28   Reid A. Bryson and Robert U. Bryson. "The History of Woodland Climatic Environments: As Simulated with Archaeoclimatic Models." Paper presented at the Joint Midwest and Plains Archaeological Conference, St. Paul, Minnesota, 2000.

CHAPTER THREE

1   Robert A. Birmingham and Leslie E. Eisenberg, *Indian Mounds of Wisconsin* (Madison: University of Wisconsin Press, 2000).

2   Hugh Highsmith, *The Mounds of Koshkonong and Rock River: A History of Ancient Indian Earthworks in Wisconsin* (Fort Atkinson, WI: The Fort Atkinson Historical Society-Highsmith Press, 1997).

3   Philip H. Salkin, "The Horicon and Kekoskee Phases: Cultural
     Complexity in the Late Woodland Stage in Southeastern
     Wisconsin," in *Late Woodland Societies: Tradition and
     Transformation Across the Continent,* eds. Thomas E. Emerson,
     Dale I. McElrath, and Andrew C. Fortier (Lincoln: University of
     Nebraska Press, 2000), 525–542; John D. Richards, "Collars,
     Castellations, and Cahokia: A Regional Perspective on the Aztalan
     Ceramic Assemblage," *The Wisconsin Archeologist* 84, nos. 1 & 2
     (2003): 139–154.

4   John Martin Kelly, "Delineating the Spatial and Temporal
     Boundaries of Late Woodland Collared Wares from Wisconsin and
     Illinois" (Master's thesis, University of Wisconsin–Milwaukee,
     2002); George W. Christiansen III, "The Late Woodland Leviathan
     and Cahokia: A Regional Perspective on the Aztalan Ceramic
     Assemblage," *The Wisconsin Archeologist* 84, nos. 1 & 2 (2003):
     219–249.

5   David F. Overstreet, "Cultural Dynamics of the Late Prehistoric
     Period," in *Mounds, Modoc and Mesoamerica: Papers in Honor of
     Melvin L. Fowler,* Illinois State Museum Scientific Papers 28, ed.
     Steven R. Ahler (Springfield: Illinois State Museum, 2000),
     405–438.

6   James B. Stoltman, "A Reconsideration of Cultural Processes
     Linking Cahokia to its Northern Hinterlands During the Period
     A.D.1000–1200," in *Mounds, Modoc and Mesoamerica: Papers in
     Honor of Melvin L. Fowler,* Illinois State Museum Scientific Papers
     28, ed. Steven R. Ahler (Springfield: Illinois State Museum, 2000),
     439–455.

7.   Timothy R. Pauketat, "Refiguring the Archaeology of Greater
     Cahokia," *Journal of Archaeological Research* 6, no. 1 (1998):
     45–89.

8   John E. Kelly, "The Evidence for Prehistoric Exchange and its
     Implications for the Development of Cahokia," in *New Perspectives
     on Cahokia: Views from the Periphery,* Monographs in World
     Archaeology no. 2, ed. James B. Stoltman (Madison: Prehistory
     Press, 1991), 65–93.

9   Salzer and Rajnovich, *The Gottschall Rockshelter.*

10   Salzer and Rajnovich, *The Gottschall Rockshelter;* Hall, *Archaeology
     of the Soul,* 147–151.

11   William Green and Roland L. Rodell, "The Mississippian Presence and Cahokia Interaction at Trempealeau, Wisconsin," *American Antiquity* 59 (1994): 334–358.

12   Robert F. Boszhardt, "The Late Woodland and Middle Mississippian Component at the Iva Site, La Crosse County, Wisconsin in the Driftless Area of the Upper Mississippi Valley," *Minnesota Archaeologist* 63 (2004): 60–85; Danielle Benden, "The Fisher Mounds Site Complex: Early Middle Mississippian Exploration in the Upper Mississippi Valley," *Minnesota Archaeologist* 63 (2004): 7–24.

13   Fred A. Finney and James B. Stoltman, "The Fred Edwards Site: A Case of Stirling Phase Culture Contact in Southwestern Wisconsin," in *New Perspectives on Cahokia: Views from the Periphery*, Monographs in World Archaeology no. 2, ed. James B. Stoltman (Madison: Prehistory Press, 1991), 229–252.

14   Roland L. Rodell, "The Diamond Bluff Site Complex and Cahokia Influence in the Red Wing Locality," in *New Perspectives on Cahokia: Views from the Periphery*, Monographs in World Archaeology no. 2, ed. James B. Stoltman (Madison: Prehistory Press, 1991), 253–280.

15   Jeffery A. Behm, "An Early Mississippian Component at the Bell Site (47-Wn-9), Winnebago County, Wisconsin," (paper presented at the 48th Annual Midwest Archaeological Conference, Columbus, Ohio, October 3–6, 2002).

16   Robert Hall, *The Archaeology of Carcajou Point*, 2 Volumes, (Madison: University of Wisconsin Press, 1962).

CHAPTER FOUR

1   Lynne Goldstein and Robert Kind, "Early Vegetation in the Region," in *Southeastern Wisconsin Archaeological Project, 1986–1987, and Project Summary*, University of Wisconsin–Milwaukee Archaeological Laboratory Reports of Investigations 88 (Milwaukee, 1987), 18–37.

2   Birmingham and Eisenberg, *Indian Mounds of Wisconsin*.

3   Richards, "Ceramics and Culture at Aztalan."

4   Barrett, *Ancient Aztalan*.

5   Richards, "Ceramics and Culture at Aztalan."

6   Richards, "Ceramics and Culture at Aztalan"; James B. Stoltman, "The Role of Petrography in the Study of Archaeological Ceramics" in Earth Sciences and Archaeology, eds. P. Goldberg, V. T. Holliday and C. R. Ferring (New York: Kluwer Academic/Plenum, 2001), 297–326.

7   John R. Swanton, *Indian Tribes of the Lower Mississippi River Valley and Adjacent Coast of the Gulf of Mexico*. Smithsonian Institution, Bureau of Ethnology Bulletin 43 (Washington, D.C., 1911).

8   Edward G. Bourne, *Narratives of the Career of the Hernando de Soto* (New York: A. S. Barnes and Co., 1904), vol. 2: 115.

9   Richards, "Ceramics and Culture at Aztalan."

10   Ibid.

11   Swanton, *Indian Tribes of the Lower Mississippi River Valley,* 113

12   Le Page Du Pratz, *Histoire de la Louisiane.*

13   Lewis, Stout, and Wesson, "The Design of Mississippian Towns."

14   Goldstein and Freeman, "Aztalan: A Middle Mississippian Village."

15   Garcilaso de la Vega, "La Florida," in *The De Soto Chronicles: The Expedition of Hernando de Soto to North America in 1539–1543,* trans. Charmion Shelby, eds. L. A. Clayton, V. J. Knight Jr., and E. C. Moore (Tuscaloosa: University of Alabama Press, 1993), vol. 2: 186.

16   Goldstein and Gaff, "Recasting the Past."

17   Bourne, *Narratives of the Career of the Hernando de Soto,* vol. 1: 27–28.

18   Robert F. Maher, "The Excavation and Reconstruction of the Southwest Pyramidal Mound at Aztalan," *The Wisconsin Archeologist* 39, no. 1 (1958): 77–101.

19   Rowe, "A Crematorium at Aztalan."

20   Lapham, *The Antiquities of Wisconsin,* 47.

21   Thomas E. Emerson and Timothy R. Pauketat, "Embodying Power and Resistance in Cahokia," in *Dynamics of Power,* Center for Archaeological Investigations, Occasional Paper 30, ed. M. O'Donovan (Carbondale: Southern Illinois University, 2002), 105–125.

22   James Scherz, *Wisconsin's Effigy Mounds* (Madison: The Ancient Earthworks Society, 1991.

23   Robert Boszhardt, Mississippi Valley Archaeology Center, personal communication, 2003.

CHAPTER FIVE

1   Richards, "Ceramics and Culture at Aztalan"; Richards, "Collars, Castellations, and Cahokia."

2   Goldstein and Freeman, "Aztalan: A Middle Mississippian Village"; Lynne Goldstein, Robert Cook, and Peter Cunningham, "Aztalan Research: Preparing for Park Interpretation and Planning," Report submitted to the Wisconsin Department of Natural Resources, 1999; Matthew C. Warwick, "A Diachronic Study of Animal Exploitation at Aztalan: A Late Prehistoric Village," (Master's thesis, University of Wisconsin–Milwaukee, 2002).

3   Warwick, "A Diachronic Study of Animal Exploitation."

4   James L. Theler, "Aboriginal Utilization of Freshwater Mussels at the Aztalan Site, Wisconsin," In *Beamers, Bobwhites, and Blue-Points: Tributes to the Career of Paul W. Parmalee*, eds. Paul W. Parmalee, James R. Purdue, Walter Klippel, and Bonnie W. Styles (Springfield: Illinois State Museum Scientific Papers 23, 1991): 315–332.

5   James L. Theler and Robert F. Boszhardt, *Twelve Millennia: Archaeology of the Upper Mississippi Valley* (Iowa City: University of Iowa Press, 2003): 135–136; Robert F. Boszhardt, *Projectile Point Guide for the Upper Mississippi River Valley* (Iowa City: University of Iowa Press, 2003), 78.

6   Robert F. Boszhardt and James N. Gundersen, "X-Ray Powder Diffraction Analysis of Early and Middle Woodland Red Pipes from Wisconsin," *Midcontinental Journal of Archaeology* 28, no. 1 (2003): 33–48; Robert F. Boszhardt, "The Late Woodland and Middle Mississippian Component at the Iva Site"; John Richards, Randall Hughes, and Thomas Emerson, "Sourcing Aztalan's Ear Spools" (paper presented at the Wisconsin Archeological Survey meetings, Madison, Wisconsin, April 23, 2005).

7   Hall, *Archaeology of the Soul*, 145–154.

8   Rowe, "A Crematorium at Aztalan."

9   Emerson, *Mississippian Stone Images in Illinois;* Adam King, "Power and the Sacred: Mound C and the Etowah Chiefdom," in *Hero, Hawk, and Open Hand: American Indian Art of the Midwest and South,* eds. Richard F. Townsend and Robert V. Sharp (Chicago: The Art Institute of Chicago; New Haven: Yale University Press, 2004), 154.

10   Thomas E. Emerson, "Cahokian Elite Ideology and the Mississippian Cosmos," in *Cahokia: Domination and Ideology in the Mississippian World,* ed. Timothy R. Pauketat and Thomas E. Emerson (Lincoln: University of Nebraska Press, 1997), 190–228.

11   Young and Fowler, *Cahokia, The Great Native American Metropolis;* Witthoft, *Green Corn Ceremonialism.*

12   M. Du Mont, *Memoires Historique sur la Lousiane* (Paris: Cl. J. B. Bauche, 1753), 202–203.

13   Salkin, "The Horicon and Kekoskee Phases," 537.

14   Richards, "Ceramics and Culture at Aztalan."

15   Young and Fowler, *Cahokia, The Great Native American Metropolis,* 294.

16   Robert F. Maher and David Baerreis, "The Aztalan Lithic Complex," *The Wisconsin Archeologist* 39, no. 1 (1958): 24; Barrett, *Ancient Aztalan,* 77–101.

17   David F. Overstreet, "Oneota Prehistory and History," *The Wisconsin Archeologist* 78, nos. 1 & 2 (1997): 250–297; Robert Jeske, "Crescent Bay Hunt Club: Radiocarbon Dates and Research Summary," in *Program in Midwestern Archaeology (Southeastern Wisconsin Archaeology Program): 2000–2001,* Archaeological Research Laboratory Report of Investigations 148, ed. R. J. Jeske (Milwaukee: University of Wisconsin–Milwaukee, 2001), 4–12; J. D. Richards and R. J. Jeske, "Location, Location, Location: The Temporal and Cultural Context of Late Prehistoric Settlement in Southeast Wisconsin." *The Wisconsin Archeologist* 83, no. 2 (2002), 32–54; Richards, "Ceramics and Culture at Aztalan."

18   Overstreet, "Cultural Dynamics of the Late Prehistoric Period," 433; Richards and Jeske, "Location, Location, Location," 45.

19   Christy G. Turner and Jacqueline A. Turner, *Man Corn* (Salt Lake City: University of Utah Press, 1999).

20   Goldstein and Freeman, "Aztalan: A Middle Mississippian Village"; George W. Christiansen III, "Warfare, Torture and Cannibalism: A Slice of Life on the Northern Frontier of the Middle Mississippian" (paper presented at the Midwest Archaeological and Plains Anthropological Conference, St. Paul, Minnesota, November, 2000).

21   Kristen Linnea Anderson, "The Aztalan Site Skeletal Inventory and Excavation History" (Master's thesis, University of Chicago, 1994).

22   Bruce Trigger, *The Children of the Aataentsic: A History of the Huron People to 1660*. 2 vols. (Montreal: McGill-Queens University Press, 1976).

23   Gerald F. Schroedl, "Mississippian Towns in the Eastern Tennessee Valley," in *Mississippian Towns and Sacred Places: Searching for an Architectural Grammar."* ed. R. Barry Lewis and Charles Stout (Tuscaloosa, Alabama: University of Alabama Press, 1998), 89; William W. Baden, "A Dynamic Model of Stability in Mississippian Agricultural Systems" (PhD dissertation, University of Tennessee, Knoxville, 1987).

24   Barrett, *Ancient Aztalan*, 415, Plate 6.

25   Charles E. Brown papers, Box 29, Wisconsin Historical Society Archives, Madison.

CHAPTER SIX

1   W. C. McKern, "Aztalan," *The Wisconsin Archeologist* 27 (1946): 52.

2   Hyer, "Ruins of the Ancient City of Aztalan."

3   Lapham, *The Antiquities of Wisconsin*, 50.

4   McKern, "Aztalan."

5   Wisconsin Department of Natural Resources, Historic Sites Task Force, Final Report, Wisconsin Department of Natural Resources, Madison, May 26, 1989.

6   Goldstein, Cook, and Cunningham, "Aztalan Research."

Bibliography

Anderson, Kristen Linnea. "Aztalan Site: A Human Skeletal Inventory and Excavation History." Master's thesis, University of Chicago, 1994.

Baden, William W. "A Dynamic Model of Stability in Mississippian Agricultural Systems." PhD dissertation, University of Tennessee, Knoxville, 1987.

Baerreis, David A. and Joan E. Freeman. "Late Woodland Pottery as Seen from Aztalan." *The Wisconsin Archeologist* 39, no. 1 (1958): 35–61.

Barrett, Samuel A. *Ancient Aztalan*. Bulletin of the Museum of the City of Milwaukee 13 (1933).

Behm, Jeffery. "An Early Mississippian Component at the Bell Site (47-Wn-9), Winnebago County, Wisconsin." Paper presented at the 48th Annual Midwest Archaeological Conference, Columbus, Ohio, October 3–6, 2002.

Benden, Danielle. "The Fisher Mounds Site Complex: Early Middle Mississippian Exploration in the Upper Mississippi Valley." *Minnesota Archaeologist* 63 (2004): 7–24.

Birmingham, Robert A. and Leslie E. Eisenberg. *Indian Mounds of Wisconsin*. Madison: University of Wisconsin Press, 2000.

Boszhardt, Robert F. "Oneota Horizons: A La Crosse Perspective." *The Wisconsin Archeologist* 49, no. 1 (1998): 196–226.

———. *Projectile Point Guide for the Upper Mississippi River Valley*. Iowa City: University of Iowa Press, 2003.

———. "The Late Woodland and Middle Mississippian Component at the Iva Site, La Crosse County, Wisconsin in the Driftless Area of the Upper Mississippi Valley." *Minnesota Archaeologist* 63 (2004): 60–85.

Boszhardt, Robert F. and James Gundersen. "X-Ray Powder Diffraction Analysis of Early and Middle Woodland Red Pipes from Wisconsin." *Midcontinental Journal of Archaeology* 28, no. 1 (2003): 33–48

Bourne, Edward G. *Narratives of the Career of the Hernando de Soto.* 2 Vols. New York: Barnes, 1904.

Brose, David S., James A. Brown, and David W. Penney. *Ancient Art of the American Woodland Indians.* New York: Harry N. Abrams, Inc., 1985.

Brown, Charles E. Charles E. Brown Papers. Wisconsin Historical Society, Madison.

Brown, James A. "The Cahokia Mound 72-Sub 1 Burials as Collective Representation." *The Wisconsin Archeologist* 84, nos. 1 & 2 (2003): 81–98.

Bryson, Reid A. and Robert U. Bryson. The History of Woodland Climatic Environments: As Simulated with Archaeoclimatic Models. Paper presented at the Joint Midwest Archaeological and Plains Anthropological Conference, St. Paul, Minnesota, November, 2000.

Christiansen III, George W. "Warfare, Torture and Cannibalism: A Slice of Life on the Northern Frontier of the Middle Mississippian." Paper presented at the Joint Midwest Archaeological and Plains Anthropological Conference, St. Paul, Minnesota, November, 2000.

———. "The Late Woodland Leviathan and Cahokia: A Regional Perspective on the Aztalan Ceramic Assemblage." *The Wisconsin Archeologist* 84, nos.1 & 2 (2003): 219–249.

DeBoer, Warren R. "Like a Rolling Stone: The Chunkey Game and Political Organization in Eastern North America." *Southeastern Archaeology* 12 (1993): 83–92.

Du Mont, M. *Memoires Historique sur la Lousiane.* Paris: Cl. J. B. Bauche 1753.

Emerson, Thomas E. *Mississippian Stone Images in Illinois.* Illinois Archaeological Survey Circular 6. Urbana: Illinois Archaeological Survey, 1982.

———. "Water, Serpents, and the Underworld: An Exploration into Cahokia Symbolism." In *The Southeastern Ceremonial Complex; Artifacts and Analysis: The Cottonlandia Conference,* edited by Patricia Galloway, 45–92. Lincoln: University of Nebraska Press, 1989.

———. "Cahokian Elite Ideology and the Mississippian Cosmos." In *Cahokia: Domination and Ideology in the Mississippian World,* edited by Timothy R. Pauketat and Thomas E. Emerson, 190–228. Lincoln: University of Nebraska Press, 1997.

Emerson, Thomas E. and Timothy R. Pauketat. "Embodying Power and Resistance in Cahokia." In *Dynamics of Power.* Center for Archaeological Investigations, Occasional Paper 30, ed. by M. O'Donovan, 105–125. Carbondale: Southern Illinois University, 2002.

Finney, Fred A. and James B. Stoltman. "The Fred Edwards Site: A Case of Stirling Phase Cultural Contact in Southwestern Wisconsin." In *New Perspectives on Cahokia: Views from the Periphery.* Monographs in World Archaeology no. 2, ed. James Stoltman, 229–252. Madison: Prehistory Press, 1991.

Fowler, Melvin, Jerome Rose, Barbara Vander Leest, and Steven R. Ahler. *The Mound 72 Area: Dedicated and Sacred Space in Early Cahokia.* Illinois State Museum Reports of Investigations no. 54. Springfield: Illinois State Museum, 1999.

Goldstein, Lynne. "The Implications of Aztalan's Location." In *New Perspectives on Cahokia: Views from the Periphery.* Monographs in World Archaeology no. 2, ed. James B. Stoltman, 209–228. Madison: Prehistory Press, 1991.

———. "Mississippian Ritual as Viewed Through the Practice of Secondary Disposal of the Dead." In *Mounds, Modoc, and Mesoamerica: Papers in Honor of Melvin L. Fowler.* Illinois State Museum Scientific Papers 28, ed. Steven R. Ahler, 193–207. Springfield: Illinois State Museum, 2000.

Goldstein, Lynne, Robert Cook, and Peter Cunningham. "Aztalan Research: Preparing for Park Interpretation and Planning." Report submitted to the Wisconsin Department of Natural Resources, 1999.

Goldstein, Lynne and Joan Freeman. "Aztalan: A Middle Mississippian Village." *The Wisconsin Archeologist* 79, nos. 1 & 2 (1997): 223–248.

Goldstein, Lynne and Donald H. Gaff. "Recasting the Past: Examining Assumptions about Aztalan." *The Wisconsin Archeologist* 83, no. 2 (2002): 98–110.

Goldstein, Lynne and Robert Kind. "Early Vegetation in the Region." In *Southeastern Wisconsin Archaeological Project, 1986–1987, and Project Summary.* Archaeological Laboratory Reports of Investigations 88, ed. Lynne Goldstein, 18–37. Milwaukee: University of Wisconsin–Milwaukee, 1987.

Goldstein, Lynne and John D. Richards. "Ancient Aztalan: The Cultural and Ecological Context of a Late Prehistoric Site in the Midwest." In *Cahokia and the Hinterlands: Middle Mississippian Cultures of the Midwest,* edited by Thomas E. Emerson and R. Barry Lewis, 193–206. Urbana: University of Illinois Press, 1991.

Green, William and Roland L. Rodell. "The Mississippian Presence and Cahokia Interaction at Trempealeau, Wisconsin." *American Antiquity* 59 (1994): 334–358.

Hall, Robert. *The Archaeology of Carcajou Point,* 2 Vols. Madison: University of Wisconsin Press, 1962.

———. *Archaeology of the Soul: North American Belief and Ritual.* Urbana: University of Illinois Press, 1997.

Hedman, Kristin and Eve A. Hargrave. *Hill Prairie Mounds: The Osteology of a Late Middle Mississippian Mortuary Population.* Transportation Archaeological Reports 6. University of Illinois-Urbana: Illinois Transportation Archaeological Research Program, 1999.

Highsmith, Hugh. *The Mounds of Koshkonong and Rock River: A History of Ancient Indian Earthworks in Wisconsin.* Fort Atkinson, WI: The Fort Atkinson Historical Society-Highsmith Press, 1997.

Hudson, Charles M. *The Southeastern Indians.* Knoxville: University of Tennessee Press, 1976.

Hyer, Nathaniel F. "Ruins of the Ancient City of Aztalan." *Milwaukee Advertiser,* February, 1837.

Jeske, Robert J. "Crescent Bay Hunt Club: Radiocarbon Dates and Research Summary." In *Program in Midwestern Archaeology (Southeastern Wisconsin Archaeology Program): 2000–2001*. Archaeological Research Laboratory Report of Investigations 148, ed. R. J. Jeske, 4–12. Milwaukee: University of Wisconsin–Milwaukee, 2001.

Kaufman, Kira E. and William F. Kean. "Archaeological Spatial Analysis at Aztalan State Park (47JE1): Using Geophysical Techniques to Interpret Prehistoric Landscape Features." *The Wisconsin Archeologist* 83 (2002): 111–112.

Kelly, John E. "The Evidence for Prehistoric Exchange and Its Implications for the Development of Cahokia." In *New Perspectives on Cahokia: Views from the Periphery*. Monographs in World Archaeology, no. 2, edited by James B. Stoltman, 65–93. Madison: Prehistory Press, 1991.

Kelly, John Martin. "Delineating the Spatial and Temporal Boundaries of Late Woodland Collared Wares from Wisconsin and Illinois." Master's thesis, University of Wisconsin–Milwaukee, 2002.

King, Adam. "Power and the Sacred: Mound C and the Etowah Chiefdom." n *Hero, Hawk, and Open Hand: American Indian Art of the Midwest and South,* edited by Richard F. Townsend and Robert V. Sharp, 151–165. Chicago: The Art Institute of Chicago; New Haven: Yale University Press, 2004.

Lapham, Increase A. *The Antiquities of Wisconsin, As Surveyed and Described.* 1855. Reprint, with a foreword by Robert A. Birmingham and introduction by Robert P. Nurre, Madison: University of Wisconsin Press, 2001.

———. Papers. Wisconsin Historical Society, Madison, Wisconsin.

Le Page Du Pratz, Antoine-Simon. *Histoire de la Louisiane.* Paris: De Bure, 1758.

Lewis, R. Barry, Charles Stout, and Cameron B. Wesson. "The Design of Mississippian Towns." In *Mississippian Towns and Sacred Places: Searching for an Architectural Grammar,*" edited by R. Barry Lewis and Charles Stout, 1–21. Tuscaloosa, Alabama: University of Alabama Press, 1998.

Lewis, Theodore H. "The 'Aztalan' Enclosure Newly Described." *American Antiquarian and Oriental Journal* 16 (1894): 205–208.

Maher, Robert F. "Excavation and Reconstruction of the Southwest Pyramidal Mound at Aztalan." *The Wisconsin Archeologist* 39, no. 1 (1958): 77–101.

Maher, Robert F. and David A. Baerreis. "The Aztalan Lithic Complex." *The Wisconsin Archeologist* 39, no. 1 (1958): 5–26.

McKern, W.C. "Aztalan." *The Wisconsin Archeologist* 27 (1946): 41–52.

Mink, Claudia Gellam. *Cahokia: City of the Sun*. Collinsville, IL: Cahokia Mounds Museum Society, 1992.

Ollendorf, Amy L. "Changing Landscapes in the American Bottom (USA): An Interdisciplinary Investigation with an Emphasis on the Late Prehistoric and Early Historic Periods." PhD dissertation, University of Minnesota-Minneapolis, 1993: 175.

Overstreet, David F. "Oneota Prehistory and History." *The Wisconsin Archeologist* 78, nos. 1 & 2 (1997): 250–297.

———. "Cultural Dynamics of the Late Prehistoric Period." In *Mounds, Modoc and Mesoamerica: Papers in Honor of Melvin L. Fowler*. Illinois State Museum Scientific Papers 28, ed. Steven R. Ahler, 405–438. Springfield: Illinois State Museum, 2000.

Parmalee, Paul W. "Animal Remains from the Aztalan Site, Jefferson County, Wisconsin." *The Wisconsin Archeologist* 41 (1960): 1–10.

Pauketat, Timothy R. "Refiguring the Archaeology of Greater Cahokia." *Journal of Archaeological Research* 6, no. 1 (1998): 45–89.

———. *Ancient Cahokia and the Mississippians*. Cambridge: University of Cambridge Press, 2004.

Peet, Stephen D. "Emblematic Mounds in Wisconsin; The Forms They Represent." *Wisconsin Historical Collections* 9 (1882): 40–74.

Radin, Paul. *The Winnebago Tribe*. 1923. Reprint, Lincoln: University of Nebraska Press, 1990.

Richards, John D. "Ceramics and Culture at Aztalan: A Late Prehistoric Village in Southeast Wisconsin." PhD dissertation, University of Wisconsin–Milwaukee, 1992.

———. "Collars, Castellations, and Cahokia: A Regional Perspective on the Aztalan Ceramic Assemblage." *The Wisconsin Archaeologist* 84, nos. 1 & 2 (2003): 139–155.

Richards, John D., Randall Hughes, and Thomas Emerson, "Sourcing Aztalan's Ear Spools." Paper presented at the Wisconsin Archeological Survey meeting, Madison, Wisconsin, April 23, 2005.

Richards, John D. and Robert J. Jeske. "Location, Location, Location: The Temporal and Cultural Context of Late Prehistoric Settlement in Southeast Wisconsin." *The Wisconsin Archeologist* 83, no. 2 (2002): 32–54.

Ritzenthaler, Robert, ed. "Aztalan: Exploration and Reconstruction," *The Wisconsin Archaeologist* 39, no. 1 (1958)

Rodell, Roland L. "The Diamond Bluff Site Complex and Cahokia Influence in the Red Wing Locality." In *New Perspectives on Cahokia: Views from the Periphery*. Monographs in World Archaeology no. 2, ed. James B. Stoltman, 253–280. Madison: Prehistory Press, 1991.

Rowe, Chandler W. "A Crematorium at Aztalan." *The Wisconsin Archeologist* 39, no. 1 (1958): 101–110.

Salkin, Philip. "The Horicon and Kekoskee Phases: Cultural Complexity in the Late Woodland Stage in Southeastern Wisconsin." In *Late Woodland Societies: Tradition and Transformation Across the Continent,* edited by Thomas E. Emerson, Dale I. McElrath, and Andrew C. Fortier, 525–542. Lincoln: University of Nebraska Press, 2000.

Salzer, Robert and Grace Rajnovich. *The Gottschall Rockshelter: An Archaeological Mystery.* St. Paul: Prairie Smoke Press, 2000.

Scherz, James. *Wisconsin's Effigy Mounds.* Madison: The Ancient Earthworks Society, 1991.

Schroedl, Gerald F. "Mississippian Towns in the Eastern Tennessee Valley." In *Mississippian Towns and Sacred Places: Searching for an Architectural Grammar,* edited by R. Barry Lewis and Charles Stout, 64–92. Tuscaloosa, Alabama: University of Alabama Press, 1998.

Sterling, William. T. "A Visit to Aztalan in 1838." *The Wisconsin Archeologist* 19, no. 1 (1920): 18–19.

Stevenson, Katherine P., Robert F. Boszhardt, Charles R. Moffat, Philip H. Salkin, Thomas C. Pleger, James L. Theler, and Constance M. Arzigian. "The Woodland Stage." *The Wisconsin Archeologist* 78, nos. 1 & 2 (1997): 140–201.

Stoltman, James B. "A Reconsideration of the Cultural Processes Linking Cahokia to Its Northern Highlands During the Period A.D. 1000–1200." In *Mounds, Modoc, and Mesoamerica: Papers in Honor of Melvin L. Fowler.* Illinois State Museum Scientific Papers 28, ed. Steve Ahler, 439–454. Springfield: Illinois State Museum, 2000.

———. "The Role of Petrography in the Study of Archaeological Ceramics." In *Earth Sciences and Archaeology,* edited by P.Goldberg, V. T. Holliday and C. R Ferring, 297–326. New York: Kluwer Academic/Plenum, 2001.

Stoltman, James B. and George W. Christiansen. "The Late Woodland Stage in the Driftless Area of the Upper Mississippi Valley." In *Late Woodland Societies: Tradition and Transformation Across the Continent,* edited by Thomas E. Emerson, Dale I. McElrath, and Andrew C. Fortier, 497–524. Lincoln: University of Nebraska Press, 2000.

Stout, Charles and R. Barry Lewis. "Mississippian Towns in Kentucky." In *Mississippian Towns and Sacred Places: Searching for an Architectural Grammar,* edited by R. Barry Lewis and Charles Stout, 151–178. Tuscaloosa, Alabama: University of Alabama Press, 1998.

Stuebe, Fred K. "Site Survey and Test Excavations in the Aztalan Area." *The Wisconsin Archeologist* 57, no. 4 (1976): 198–259.

Swanton, John R. *Indian Tribes of the Lower Mississippi River Valley and Adjacent Coast of the Gulf of Mexico.* Smithsonian Institution, Bureau of Ethnology Bulletin 43, Washington, D.C., 1911.

―――. *Religious Beliefs and Medicinal Practices of the Creek Indians.* Smithsonian Institution, Annual Report of the Bureau of American Ethnology. Washington, D.C., 1928.

Theler, James L. "Aboriginal Utilization of Freshwater Mussels at the Aztalan Site, Wisconsin." In *Beamers, Bobwhites, and Blue-Points: Tributes to the Career of Paul W. Parmalee.* Illinois State Museum Scientific Papers 23, eds. Paul W. Parmalee, James R. Purdue, Walter Klippel, and Bonnie W. Styles, 315–332. Springfield: Illinois State Museum, 1991.

Theler, James L. and Robert F. Boszhardt. *Twelve Millennia: Archaeology of the Upper Mississippi Valley.* Iowa City: University of Iowa Press, 2003.

Trigger, Bruce. *The Children of the Aataentsic: A History of the Huron People to 1660.* 2 vols. Montreal: McGill-Queens University Press, 1976.

Turner, Christy G. and Jacqueline A. Turner. *Man Corn.* Salt Lake City: University of Utah Press, 1999.

Vega, Garcilaso de la. "La Florida" In *The De Soto Chronicles: The Expedition of Hernando de Soto to North America in 153–1543,* Vol. 2, translated by Charmion Shelby and edited by L. A. Clayton, V. J. Knight Jr., and E. C. Moore, 25–559. Tuscaloosa, Alabama: University of Alabama Press, 1993.

Warwick, Matthew C. "A Diachronic Study of Animal Exploitation at Aztalan: A Late Prehistoric Village." Master's thesis, University of Wisconsin–Milwaukee, 2002.

West, George A. "The Indian Authorship of Wisconsin Antiquities." *The Wisconsin Archeologist* O.S. 6, no. 4 (1907): 167–256.

Wisconsin Department of Natural Resources. Historic Sites Task Force, Final Report, Wisconsin Department of Natural Resources, Madison, May 26, 1989.

Witthoft, John. *Green Corn Ceremonialism in the Eastern Woodlands.* Occasional Contributions from the Museum of Anthropology of the University of Michigan 13, 1949.

Young, Biloine Whiting and Melvin L. Fowler. *Cahokia, The Great Native American Metropolis.* Urbana: University of Illinois Press, 2000.

Illustration Credits

Contents page: Painting by Rob Evans, used with permission of the Kenosha Public Museum

INTRODUCTION

Figure A: Photograph by Joel Heiman

Figure B: Illustration from *Ancient Aztalan,* used with permission of the Milwaukee Public Museum

Figure C: Lynne Goldstein, Department of Anthropology, Michigan State University

CHAPTER ONE

Figure 1.1a: Washington, D.C.: Smithsonian Institution, 1855

Figure 1.1b: Illustration from *Antiquities of Wisconsin*, used with permission of the Wisconsin Historical Society

Figure 1.2: Courtesy of the Milwaukee Public Museum

Figure 1.3: Wisconsin Historical Society Image ID WHi 36713

Figure 1.4: Courtesy of the Milwaukee Public Museum, Neg. No. 32081

Figure 1.5: Courtesy of the Milwaukee Public Museum

Figure 1.6a: Photograph courtesy of Wisconsin Archeological Survey

Figure 1.6b: Museum Archaeology Program, Wisconsin Historical Society

Figure 1.6c: Museum Archaeology Program, Wisconsin Historical Society

Figures 1.7 and 1.8: Photograph by Lynne Goldstein, Department of Anthropology, Michigan State University

Figures 1.9a & b: Photograph by Tom Davies, Wisconsin Department of Natural Resources

CHAPTER TWO

Figure 2.1: Painting by William Iseminger, courtesy of the Cahokia Mounds Historic Site

Figure 2.2: Le Page Du Pratz, *Historie de la Louisiane,* Paris, 1758

Figure 2.3: Map by Amelia Janes

Figure 2.4: Courtesy of the National Museum of the American Indian, Smithsonian Institution

Figure 2.5: Used with permission from University of Arkansas Museum Collections, Cat. No. 47-2-1. Photograph courtesy of Illinois Transportation Archaeological Research Program, University of Illinois

Figures 2.6a & b: Courtesy of the Illinois Transportation Archaeological Research Program, University of Illinois

Figure 2.7: Courtesy of the Milwaukee Public Museum

Figure 2.8: Illustrations by Lloyd Kenneth Townsend, courtesy of the Cahokia Mounds Historic Site

Figure 2.9: Drawing reproduced from Lapham's *Antiquities of Wisconsin*

Figure 2.10: National Museum of the American Indian, Smithsonian Institution, Washington, D.C. Photograph courtesy of the Illinois Transportation Archaeological Research Program, University of Illinois.

CHAPTER THREE

Figure 3.1: Map by Amelia Janes

Figures 3.2a &b: Woodland Madison Ware pottery photo by Robert Granflaten. Woodland collared pottery found at Aztalan courtesy of the Milwaukee Public Museum.

Figure 3.3: Photo courtesy of the Museum Archaeology Program, Wisconsin Historical Society

Figure 3.4: Drawings by Richard Dolan

Figure 3.5: Drawing by Mary Steinhauer, courtesy of Cultural Landscape Legacies.

Figure 3.6: Wisconsin Historical Society Image ID WHi (X3) 51038

CHAPTER FOUR

Figure 4.1: Map by Amelia Janes

Figures 4.2a &c: Photos by Tom Davies, Wisconsin Department of Natural Resources

Figure 4.2b: Museum Archaeology Program, Wisconsin Historical Society

Figure 4.3: Used with permission of the University of Alabama

Figures 4.4 & 4.5: Base map by Eric Paulson, used with permission of the University of Wisconsin–Milwaukee Department of Anthropology

Figure 4.5: Used with permission of the Milwaukee Public Museum

Figure 4.6: Wisconsin Historical Society collections

Figure 4.7: Base map by Eric Paulson, used with permission of the University of Wisconsin–Milwaukee Department of Anthropology

Figure 4.8: Courtesy of the Wisconsin Archeological Society

Figure 4.9: Painting by Rob Evans, used with permission of the Kenosha Public Museum

Figure 4.10: Used with permission of the Milwaukee Public Museum

Figure 4.11: Used with permission of John Richards

Figure 4.12: Wisconsin Historical Society museum drawing adapted by Laurel Fletcher

Figure 4.13: Illustration from *Ancient Aztalan* used with permission of the Milwaukee Public Museum

Figure 4.14: Base map by Eric Paulson, used with permission of the University of Wisconsin–Milwaukee Department of Anthropology

Figure 4.15: Photograph by Lynne Goldstein, Department of Anthropology, Michigan State University

Figure 4.16: Base map by Eric Paulson, used with permission of the University of Wisconsin–Milwaukee Department of Anthropology

Figure 4.17: Illustration from *Ancient Aztalan,* used with permission of the Milwaukee Public Museum

Figures 4.18 and 4.19: Photographs by Joel Heiman

Figure 4.20: Courtesy of the Wisconsin Archeological Society

Figure 4.21: Base map by Eric Paulson, used with permission of the University of Wisconsin–Milwaukee Department of Anthropology

Figure 4.22: Painting by Rob Evans, used with permission of the Kenosha Public Museum

Figure 4.23: Detail from Increase Lapham map from *Antiquities of Wisconsin,* used with permission of the Wisconsin Historical Society

Figure 4.24: University of Wisconsin Department of Geography Map Library

Figure 4.25: Photograph by Joel Heiman

Figures 4.26a, b, & c: Illustration from *Ancient Aztalan* used with permission of the Milwaukee Public Museum

Figure 4.27: Photograph by Joel Heiman

CHAPTER FIVE

Figure 5.1: Used with permission of the Milwaukee Public Museum and the Wisconsin Archaeological Society

Figure 5.2: Wisconsin Historical Society collections, photograph by Joel Heiman, WHS Museum JE1-68 300R98-1

Figure 5.3: Courtesy of the Milwaukee Public Museum

Figure 5.4a: Wisconsin Historical Society collections, photograph by Joel Heiman, WHS Museum JE-1-67 E-H1-F-1

Figure 5.4b: Wisconsin Historical Society collections, photograph by Joel Heiman, WHS Museum JE1-64 Plow Zone-1 (large awl); WHS Museum JE1-64 F17-229 (small awl)

Figure 5.4c: Wisconsin Historical Society collections, photograph by Joel Heiman, WHS Museum JE1-68-PZ21

Figure 5.4d: Lake Mills-Aztalan Historical Society museum collections, photograph by Joel Heiman

Figure 5.5: Lake Mills-Aztalan Historical Society museum collections, photograph by Joel Heiman

Figure 5.6: Lake Mills-Aztalan Historical Society museum collections, photograph by Joel Heiman

Figure 5.7: Lake Mills-Aztalan Historical Society museum collections, photograph by Joel Heiman

Figure 5.8: Illustration from *Ancient Aztalan,* used with permission of the Milwaukee Public Museum.

Figure 5.9a: Illustration from *Cahokia and the Hinterlands,* courtesy of University of Illinois Press

Figure 5.9b: Used with permission of the Milwaukee Public Museum, photograph courtesy of John Richards

Figure 5.10: Courtesy of Milwaukee Public Museum

Figure 5.11: Courtesy of the Illinois Transportation Archaeological Research Program, University of Illinois

Figure 5.12: Photo by David H. Dye, courtesy of Etowah Indian Mounds State Historic Site

Figure 5.13: Lake Mills-Aztalan Historical Society museum collections

Figure 5.14: Increase Lapham papers, Wisconsin Historical Society

CHAPTER SIX

Figure 6.1: Photograph by Joel Heiman

Figures 6.2a & b: Photographs by Tom Davies, Wisconsin Department of Natural Resources

Index

———◆•◆•◆———

References to illustrations are in italic type.

A

aerial photography, 66, *78*

agriculture, 20, 49; at Aztalan, xi, *xii,* 77, 88, 102; corn, 20, 52, 96; crops, 30; disturbance of site by modern, 2–3, 62, 77, 104; Green Corn ceremony, 10, 28–29, 31, 81, 96–97; Late Woodland civilization and, 39; lifestyle changes and, 43; tools for, 90, *90,* 91

alignment: with cardinal directions, 26, 53, 71; solar orientation of structures, 23, 70, 71–73, 81

ancestor veneration, 35, 101. *See also* mortuary practices

Ancient Aztalan (Barrett), 7, 51, 80–81, 96

The Antiquities of Wisconsin (Lapham), 2, 104

archaeology: amateur archaeology, 7

archeology: remote sensing surveys, *18,* 18–19, 76. *See also* excavations

arrowheads, 30, 91–93, *92*

Aztalan, *ix,* 83; abandonment of, *xi,* 11, 53, 101–102; agriculture at, *xi–xii,* 16, 77, 88, 102; building episodes at, 55; burning of site, 102; Cahokia linked to, 10, 43–44, 52, 85; as ceremonial site, 51; discovery and early records of, *ix,* 1; establishment of, *xi,* 47; location of, *48,* 48–49; name origins, *x,* 1; population of, *xi,* 60; preservation efforts, *xiii,* 11, 103–107; settler's village at site of, 1; simultaneous occupation by Late Woodland and Mississippian cultures, 10, 11–13, 46–47, 77, 98; springs at location, 50. *See also*

structures and architecture of Aztalan

Aztalan State Park, 103–107

B

Baerreis, David, 11

Barrett, Samuel, 6, 7–11, *8,* 51, 60, 71, 75–76, *78,* 79–81, 83, 95, 102; cannibalism thesis of, 10–11, 100; maps drawn by, *6, 69*

Behm, Jeffery, 47

beliefs and cosmology: bird/serpent dichotomy, 25; ceremonial life at Aztalan, 51, 96–98; effigy mounds and, 39; Green Corn ceremony, 10, 28–29, 31, 81, 96–97; of Late Woodland civilization, 39; post mounds, 79–81; Red Horn, 27–28, *44,* 44–45, 94; reflected in physical layout of towns, 53–55; rocks buried in mounds, 81–82; sun, importance of, 26, 29, 70, 81; water in, 39

Bell site, 47

Berlin, Hamilton-Brooks site near, 46–47

"birdman" burial, 26, 82

Birger figurine, BBB Motor site (Illinois), *28,* 29

bison, 43

bundle burials, 2, 35, 64, 72, 78, 101

burials. *See* mortuary practices

Busk. *See* Green Corn ceremony

C

Cahokia, *x–xi,* 12, 20–23, *21;* abandonment of, 35–36, 101; Aztalan linked to, 10, 43–44, 52, 85; maps showing location relative to

Robert A. Birmingham served for many years as Wisconsin State Archaeologist. He is the recipient of the Elizabeth A. Steinberg prize for his book, *Indian Mounds of Wisconsin,* co-authored with Leslie E. Eisenberg, and now teaches at University of Wisconsin–Waukesha and writes from his home in Madison.

Lynne G. Goldstein is professor and chairperson of the Department of Anthropology, Michigan State University. She has conducted field research at and around Aztalan for nearly thirty years.